THE OLD VIC

Richard Armitage

the CRUCIBLE

ARTHUR MILLER

PERFORMED IN THE ROUND
21 JUNE – 13 SEPTEMBER

COMING SOON
ELECTRA

Kristin Scott Thomas and director **Ian Rickson** reunite to bring **Sophocles'** tragedy to
The Old Vic in the round, in a version by **Frank McGuinness**. 22 Sep – 20 Dec.

A co-production with Sonia Friedman Productions.

oldvictheatre.com
0844 871 7628

The Old Vic
Season Sponsor

Bank of America
Merrill Lynch

THE CQS SPACE
The Old Vic in the round

Partnering
The Old Vic

pwc

Lizzy Disney

lizzydisney.co.uk

NOMOS
GLASHÜTTE

In support of

MÉDECINS SANS FRONTIÈRES
DOCTORS WITHOUT BORDERS

Time for life—with two limited edition timepieces in support of Doctors Without Borders/Médecins Sans Frontières. Each watch raises 100 USD, GBP, or EUR for the Nobel Peace Prize winning humanitarian organization. And still these hand-crafted mechanical watches with the red 12 cost the same as the classic models from NOMOS Glashütte. Help now, wear forever.

Funds raised are donated to Médecins Sans Frontières USA, UK, or Germany, depending on the specific model purchased. For MSF UK, the registered charity no. is 1026588. Available at selected retailers in the three participating countries, as well as online. Find your nearest NOMOS retailer at **nomos-watches.com** or order online at **nomos-store.com**

GRANTA

12 Addison Avenue, London WII 4QR | email editorial@granta.com
To subscribe go to www.granta.com, or call 845-267-3031 (toll-free 866-438-6150)
in the United States, 020 8955 7011 in the United Kingdom

ISSUE 128: SUMMER 2014

PUBLISHER AND EDITOR	Sigrid Rausing
MANAGING EDITOR	Yuka Igarashi
ONLINE AND POETRY EDITOR	Rachael Allen
DESIGNER	Daniela Silva
EDITORIAL ASSISTANTS	Louise Scothern, Francisco Vilhena
MARKETING AND SUBSCRIPTIONS	David Robinson
PUBLICITY	Aidan O'Neill
TO ADVERTISE CONTACT	Kate Rochester, katerochester@granta.com
FINANCE	Morgan Graver
SALES	Iain Chapple, Katie Hayward
IT MANAGER	Mark Williams
PRODUCTION ASSOCIATE	Sarah Wasley
PROOFS	David Atkinson, Katherine Fry Jessica Rawlinson, Vimbai Shire
CONTRIBUTING EDITORS	Daniel Alarcón, Mohsin Hamid, Isabel Hilton, A.M. Homes, Janet Malcolm, Edmund White

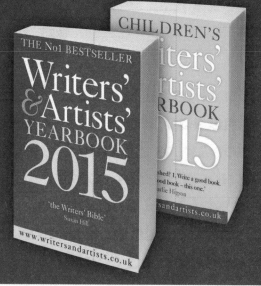

Index on Censorship
on the go

Find us in
the app store
today! A 30 day
subscription costs
just £1.79 and gives
you access to 6 years
of archived content.

Latest issue
**Brick by Brick:
Freedom 25 years
after the fall**

- Search current issue or archive
- Share pages instantly via email, Twitter, Facebook and other social networks
- Pinch or double-tap pages to zoom
- Use animated thumbnail view to flick through pages
- Swipe page edges to flip to next/previous page
- Sync any issue to your device for offline reading (WiFi)
- Tap links to take you to websites, email addresses, references, maps
- Tap contents-page links to jump to a particular article

www.indexoncensorship.org/subscribe

CONTENTS

Introduction

When I was seventeen, in 1980, I went on an American road trip with my friend Eva Gronowitz. We bought an old Vega station wagon in New York and set off, through Florida (where I got my provisional licence), Alabama, Mississippi, Louisiana, Texas, Colorado and Arizona, to California. Our useless old car would break down at regular intervals, and people stopped to help. We picked up hitch-hikers; they invited us to stay. At a trailer park in Florida, we saw Vietnam vets throw unopened cans in the fire for the explosions. In Texas we stayed in a YMCA that was partly a halfway house, with subdued women in blue overalls and stringy hair.

I got my full driver's licence in Texas. The inspector had dodged the draft, and spent the Vietnam War in Sweden. 'I love your people,' he said, smiling benignly as I failed to parallel park for the third time. We drove on and on, Neil Diamond's 'September Morn' playing on all the radio stations from New York to California. We were so innocent. But not once did we feel afraid or threatened.

Twelve years later, the young Christopher McCandless, inspired by Henry David Thoreau, set off on his own road trip, which ended, fatally, when he walked into the wild in Alaska. Jon Krakauer wrote the book, and Sean Penn, who knows a bit about another kind of wild, made a powerful film, *Into the Wild*.

Thoreau merged the ideas of individual liberty, resistance to unjust government and living in the wild, now a somewhat dangerous notion, and not just for the individuals concerned. Andrew Motion's beautiful 'found' poem speaks of Thoreau, but every piece in this issue suggests a journey into the wild, one way or another. Most are set in rural America: Alaska, Minnesota, Idaho, New Mexico and Texas.

I had expected more metaphorical wilderness, but this is America: a genuinely wild land. The wilderness itself, however, is highly regulated, sometimes by competing interests. One quarter of all American land remains in government ownership. 'It is one of the great unspoken facts of America that the land of the free largely belongs to the state,' Adam Nicolson memorably writes.

A ny collection of writing, *Granta* too, reflects the interests of the editor more than the spirit of the age, but it's tempting nevertheless to speculate about the state of the nation. We have done it before. In 2002, *Granta* published an issue entitled 'What We Think of America'. Ian Jack, then editor, was disturbed by his sense that, post 9/11, many people thought America had 'had it coming'. It is striking how even then, before the invasion of Iraq, before the War on Terror took off in earnest, and before torture was legitimized on a dubious legal technicality, people presumed violence. America, wrote Harold Pinter in his pugnacious piece, 'knows only one language – bombs and death'.

So what language does America know now? Gentle introspection, I would say, judging by what we read. We saw several pieces about the uncanny; evidence, Freud might have argued, of 9/11 and the war dead. In the end we took only two: Diane Cook's new story 'The Mast Year', and Anne Carson's 'Krapp Hour' – the surreal poetry of Carson wrapped up in the tired glibness of a TV talk show. But death and violence, often with a sense of melancholy distance, are part of many of the other stories. America is mourning, and no wonder. ∎

Sigrid Rausing

THING WITH FEATHERS THAT PERCHES IN THE SOUL

Anthony Doerr

1. The house

I am driving my twin sons home from flag football practice. It's September, it hasn't rained in two months and seemingly half of the state of Idaho is on fire. For a week the sky has been an upturned bowl the colour of putty, the clouds indistinguishable from haze, enough smoke in the air that we taste it in our food, in our throats, in our sleep. But tonight, for some reason, as we pass St Luke's Hospital, something in the sky gives way, and a breathtaking orange light cascades across the trees, the road, the windshield. We turn onto Fort Street, the road frosted with smouldering, feverish light, and just before the stoplight on Fifth, in a grassy lot, I notice, perhaps for the first time, a little house.

It's a log cabin with a swaybacked roof and a low door, like a cottage for gnomes. A little brick chimney sticks out of its shingles. Three enamel signs stand on the south side; a stone bench hunkers on the north.

It's old. It's tiny. It seems almost to tremble in the strange, volcanic light. I have passed this house, I'm guessing, three thousand times. I have jogged past it, biked past it, driven past it. Every election for the last twelve years I voted in a theatre lobby three hundred yards from it.

And yet I've never really seen it before.

2. Jerry

A week later I'm standing outside the little house with a City Parks employee named Jerry. A plaque above the door reads THIS CABIN WAS THE FIRST HOME IN BOISE TO SHELTER WOMEN AND CHILDREN. The outer walls are striped with cracked chinking and smudged with exhaust. The ratcheting powerheads of sprinklers spatter its back with each pass. An empty green bottle of something called Übermonster Energy Brew has rolled up against its north wall.

Jerry has to try three keys before he manages to push open the front door.

Inside, it's full of old leaves and hung with the pennants of cobwebs. Little fissures of light show through the panelling.

No furniture. It smells like old paint. Through the dirty steel mesh bolted over a window I can watch cars barrel past on Fort, sedans and Suburbans and pickups, maybe every third one piloted by a sunglasses-wearing mom, a kid or two or three belted into the back seat. Any minute my own wife, ferrying my own kids to school, will come charging past.

'How many people ask to come in here to look at this?' I ask Jerry.

'In four years,' he says, 'you're the first.'

3. Boise before Boise

Take away the Capitol building, the Hoff building, the US Bank building. Take away all eighteen Starbucks, all twenty-nine playgrounds, all ten thousand street lights. Take away the parking garages, Guido's Pizza, the green belt, the fire hydrants, the cheat grass, the bridges.

It's 1863 in the newly christened Idaho Territory and we're downtown. There are rocks. Magpies. The canvases of a dozen infantry tents flutter beside a cobble-bottomed creek.

Into this rides a man named John.

John has a gnarly, foot-long beard, a wagon full of tools and a girl back in Colorado. Born in Ireland, he has sailed around the globe; he's been to London, to Calcutta, around Cape Horn; he has heard the whump of Russian artillery, saw men die, won a medal.

For years he was a sailor. Now he's a prospector.

He's something else too. He's in love.

John stops at the tents and asks the infantrymen who they are, where he is, what they call this place.

Camp Boise, they say. Boise Barracks. Fort Boise.

John unpacks his wagon. To his south a green river slides along. To his north the shadows of clouds drag over foothills. All this time he's thinking of Mary.

Mary is seventeen years old. Big-nosed, wavy-haired, as Irish as he is. Good with a needle, good at seeing into people too. Her eyes, curiously, are like the eyes of a grandmother. As if, though she's half his age, she knows more about the world than he does. She too has seen a measure of the planet: born in Cork County, sent to the New World at age nine, enrolled at a convent school in New Orleans, married a man in Philadelphia at age fifteen. Gave birth to a girl. That marriage caved in, God knows why, and Mary found John in Louisville, or John found Mary, and they got married and rode two thousand miles west into the unknown, into Colorado, and now he's here, another thousand miles farther on, in this place that is not yet a place, to look for gold.

John is almost forty years old. Try for a moment to imagine all the places he might have slept: hammocks, shanties, wickiups made of willows, the lurching holds of ships, the cold ruts of the Oregon Trail. Curled on his side next to a mountain stream with his mules hobbled and elk bugling and wolves singing and the great swarming arm of the Milky Way draped over them all.

John rolls away rocks, uproots sage. Cottonwoods are bunched along the river, plenty of them. They're lousy with caterpillars, but they're lightweight, and they're close. He cuts his logs and drags them to a flat area beside the creek and uses the blade of a broad axe to wrestle their crooked shapes into straight lines.

A simple rectangle in the sand. Three feet high, then four, then five. Into the spaces between he jams clay and leaves and sticks. He leaves two low doors and two windows to cover – for now – with paper. Later, maybe, he can put in real window-glass, if window-glass ever makes it all the way out here along two thousand miles of ruts and raids and storm.

If he's lucky. If this place is lucky.

He starts on the roof. Mary is coming from Colorado in a train of fourteen wagons. Already she could be pregnant. Already she could be close.

He fashions wooden pins for door hinges. He installs a stove. He nails fabric to the insides of the walls. Just get here, Mary. Get here before winter.

4. Hope

Three hundred yards from the spot where John O'Farrell raised what would become the first family home in Boise, my wife and I used to pick up drugs from a fertility clinic. We wanted to start a family but we weren't getting pregnant. Month after month. We went through the expected stuff: tests, doubt, despair. Then I got a chance to move from Boise to work at Princeton University for a year.

Then we got pregnant.

Then we found out it was twins.

Hope, wrote Emily Dickinson, *is the thing with feathers—*

That perches in the soul—
And sings the tune without words—
and never stops—at all.

All autumn in New Jersey we worried the pregnancy wouldn't last, biology wouldn't work, the foetuses wouldn't hang on. But they did.

When my wife went home early to Idaho for Christmas, I stood in our rented New Jersey apartment, in the shadowless grey light of a snowstorm, and let myself believe for the first time that it was actually going to happen, that in a couple of months we would open the squeaky back door and carry in two babies.

The apartment's walls were blank, its stairs were steep. It was not, I realized, ready. Was not a home.

Who hasn't prepared a welcome? Set flowers on a nightstand for a returning hospital patient? Festooned a living room for a returning soldier? Stocked a refrigerator, washed a car, laid out towels? All of this is a kind of hope, a tune without words. Hope that the beloved will arrive safely, that the beloved will feel beloved.

I stood in that little apartment in 2003 thinking of my wife, of the two unknown quantities siphoning nutrients out of her day and night. How she never complained. How she ate Fruit Roll-Ups by the dozen because they were the only food that didn't make her feel sick. Then I drove alone to a shopping mall, not something I've done before or since, and bought foot-high fabric-covered letters – A, B and C – and a night light shaped like a star and something called a Graco Pack 'n Play Playard and set it up and then stayed up till midnight trying to figure out how to fold and zip it back inside the bag it came in.

When you prepare a welcome, you prepare yourself. You prepare for the moment the beloved arrives, the moment you say: I understand you've come a long way, I understand you're taking the larger risk with your life.

You say: Here. This might be humble, this might not be the place you know. This might not be everything you dreamed of. But it's something you can call home.

5. Questions

Mary O'Farrell leaves Colorado in the summer of 1863. Lincoln is president; the Emancipation Proclamation is five months old. Across the country, in South Carolina, Union batteries are bombarding Fort Sumter and they won't let up for two years. On the long road north does she remember what it was like to be a nine-year-old girl and leave her home in Ireland? Does she remember the birds she saw at sea, and the light heaving on the immense fields of the Atlantic? Does she hear in her memory the Latin of Irish priests; the Gaelic of her parents; the terror when she showed up for her first day of school in New Orleans, and heard those accents, and saw faces that were utterly different than every face she had known before? Does she think of her first husband, and their first night together, and does she ponder the circumstances under which she – a sixteen-year-old with a newborn daughter – left him? Does she think of that decision as a failure? Or as an exercise of courage? And was it that same courage that kept her from turning back when she saw the storm-racked brow of the Rockies for the first time, and is it courage that keeps her going now, Pike's Peak at her back, her daughter at her knees, very possibly a new, second child growing in her uterus, the wagon pressing into newer, rawer country, the bench bouncing, wheels groaning – courage that keeps her from weeping at the falling darkness and the creaking trees and the unfettered miles of sage?

It takes Mary four months and four days to reach Fort Boise. Here there are no telegrams, no grocery stores, no pharmacies. There aren't even bricks.

On legs weary from the road she walks into the little house John has built for her. Stands on the dirt floor. Sees the light trapped in its paper-covered windows.

John stops beside her, or in front of her, or behind her.

How many thousands of questions must have been coursing through that little space at that moment?

Is it good enough, does she like it, did I make it all right?

Where will I cook, where will we sleep, where will I give birth?

Will I find gold and will winter be awful and how will I feed us?

Have we finally come far enough to stop moving?

6. Home

Whatever magic John threads into the walls of their house, it works. Fort Boise survives the winter; the O'Farrells survive the winter. John embarks upon a remodel: he replaces the gable ends with board and batten siding; he cuts shingles for a proper roof.

Around them civilization mushrooms. By the time the O'Farrell cabin is a year old, Boise has a population of 1,658. There are now sixty buildings, nine general stores, five saloons, three doctors and two breweries.

John buys wallpaper to cover the interior planking. He builds a fireplace from bricks.

Meanwhile, Mary does not need a fertility clinic. In the years after she arrives in Idaho, she gives birth to six more kids. She loses three. She also adopts seven children.

Their home is two hundred square feet, smaller than my bedroom. There are no SpongeBob reruns to put on when the kids get too loud. No pizzerias to call when she can't think of what to cook; there is no telephone, no freezer, no electricity. No internal plumbing. No pre-moistened baby wipes.

But it's fallacy to imagine Mary O'Farrell's years in that tiny house as unrelenting hardship. Her life was almost certainly full of laughter; without question it was full of noise and energy and sunlight. One day she convinces two passing priests to start holding Catholic Mass in her house and they celebrate Sundays there for four consecutive years.

By 1868, Boise boasts four hundred buildings. Ads in the *Tri-Weekly Statesman* from that year offer coral earrings and 18-carat-gold ladies' watches and English saucepans and hydraulic nozzles and 24-hour physicians' prescriptions. A stage line boasts that it can bring a person to San Francisco in four days.

This is no longer a place of single men: by the end of that year, Boise has two hundred children in four different schools.

Eventually John shifts from the unpredictability of crawling into mining tunnels to the rituals of farming: a more sunlit profession. Soon enough he starts construction on a colonial revival at Fourth and Franklin, a real house, made of bricks.

But before it's done, before they move in, John rides to a store downtown and buys panes of glass and carries them home and fits them into strips of wood and builds real French windows for his wife, so she can sit inside their cabin and look out, so the same golden sunshine of a summer evening that every person who has ever lived in this valley knows can fall through the glass and set parallelograms of light onto the floor.

7. Probably I'm wrong about a lot of this

Maybe John O'Farrell had some help raising the walls of his cabin. Maybe Mary hated it when she first saw it. Maybe they weren't devoted to each other the way I want to believe they were; maybe I'm trying to fashion a love story out of cobwebs and ghosts.

But listen: To live for a minimum of seven years with a minimum of seven kids in two hundred square feet with no toilet paper or Netflix or Xanax requires a certain kind of imperturbability. To adopt seven kids; to not give out when snow is sifting through cracks in the chinking; to not lose your mind when a baby is feverish and screeching and a toddler is tugging your skirts and the hairdryer wind of August is blowing 110-degree heat under your door and the mass production of electric refrigerators is still fifty-five years away – something has to hold you together through all that.

It has to be love, doesn't it? In however many of its infinite permutations?

John and Mary are married for thirty-seven years. They live to see a capitol dome raised and streetcars glide up and down the streets. Out in the world Coca-Cola and motion pictures and vacuum cleaners are invented.

On 13 May 1900, the page 8 'Local Brevities' section of the *Idaho Daily Statesman* includes the following items:

The rainfall during the 36 hours preceding
5 o'clock last evening was 1.72 inches.

The May term of the supreme court will begin
tomorrow.

Mrs. John O'Farrell is lying at death's door. The
physicians have given up all hope.

The second stanza of Emily Dickinson's poem reads like this:

And sweetest—in the gale—is heard;
And sore must be the storm—
That could abash the little bird
That kept so many warm—

Sore must be the storm indeed. John outlives Mary by only a few
months. According to his obituary,

Mr. O'Farrell was one of the pioneers of Idaho,
having come to this section in the early sixties.
He was well and favorably known throughout
Idaho and the northwest.

And then there's this:

Mr. O'Farrell's wife died last spring and he never
recovered from the blow.

8. What lasts

Through the decades the house John built for Mary has been
softened by lawn sprinklers and hammered by sun. The
cottonwood it was built from makes a weak and spongy lumber, non-

resistant to decay, prone to warping, and to keep the house from collapsing, Boiseans have had to come together every few decades and retell its story. In the early 1910s, the Daughters of the American Revolution collected $173 to move and reroof it; in the 1950s, a dance was held to raise funds; seven hundred people showed up. And at the turn of the last century, folks who live in the houses around the O'Farrell Cabin raised $52,000 to help the architect Charles Hummel repair the logs, doors, windows and roof.

And so it stands, 150 years old, the same age as the city it helped establish.

As unassuming as Boise itself. Invisible to most of us. The first family home in our city. On a given night John might have lain in here on a home-made cot dreaming of his years at sea, Anatolia, cannon-fire, the churning Pacific; four or five or six or seven kids might have been hip-to-hip under quilts, breathing in unison, their exhalations showing in the cold; owls would have been hunting in the gulches, and dogs barking in town; Mary might have been sitting up, hands in her lap, drowsing, watching stars rotate past her new windows. Out the door was Boise: place of salmon, place of gold, place to buy supper and a saddle and have the doctor stitch you up before heading back out to try to wrench another quarter-ounce of metal from the hills.

Fifteen decades have passed. It's late September now, and smoke from a dozen fires still hangs in the valley, hazing everything, as I drive to a windowless grey warehouse not too far from the O'Farrell cabin. Inside, stored in an amber-coloured gloom, are rows of fifteen-foot-high shelves loaded with artefacts. There's Native American basketry in here and antique typewriters and a covered wagon, and Nazi daggers, and scary-looking foot-powered dental equipment probably eighty years old. There are prisoners' manacles and nineteenth-century wedding gowns and optometry kits and opium scrapers brought to Idaho by Chinese miners who have been dead for more than a century.

From the arcane depths of these shelves a curatorial registrar for the Idaho State Historical Museum named Sarah retrieves four items and lays them out on white Ethafoam.

A miner's pick. A long metal spike called a miner's candlestick. A tin lantern. And an ornate wooden candlestick painted white and gold.

Each is inscribed with a little black number and looped with a paper tag. Each, Sarah tells me, belonged to the O'Farrells.

Did Mary carry this lantern into town on some winter night? Did her adopted sons carry the candlestick during Mass, sheltering its flame with one hand, like the altar boys I knew in childhood? How many times did John swing this pick, hoping to feed his family, hoping to strike gold?

All four objects sit mute in front of me – points of light dredged out of the shadows, incapable of testimony.

What lasts? Is there anything you've made in your life that will still be here 150 years from now? Is there anything on your shelves that will be tagged and numbered and kept in a warehouse like this?

What does not last, if they are not retold, are the stories. Stories need to be resurrected, revivified, reimagined; otherwise they get bundled with us into our graves: a hundred thousand of them going into the ground every hour.

Or maybe they float a while, suspended in the places we used to be, waiting, hidden in plain sight, until a day when the sky breaks and the lights come on and the right person is passing by.

Outside the warehouse, the air seems smokier than before. The sky glows an apocalyptic yellow. Beneath a locust tree at the edge of the parking lot, doves hop from foot to foot. My hands tremble on the steering wheel. I start the engine but for a long minute I cannot drive.

It's not that the stuff is still here. It's not that the house still stands. It's that someone keeps the stuff on shelves. It's that someone keeps the house standing. ∎

EXOTICS

Callan Wink

On the last day of class before summer vacation, his students –
all fifteen of them, ranging age eight to sixteen – filed out the
door saying their goodbyes. Before leaving, one of his sixth-graders,
Molly Hanchet, stopped at his desk. She had red hair and freckles
and, in five years, would likely be Park County's Fourth of July Rodeo
queen. After that she would go on to pre-med at Stanford. She had
her thumbs hooked in the straps of her backpack and she said, 'Have
a good summer, Mr Colson. I hope next year you feel better.'

She left and James was forced to ponder the implications. It had to
be bad if a sixth-grade girl could see that he was fucked.

Carina lived in a small rental cabin on the river, set back in a grove
of old cottonwoods. Once, in a windstorm, he'd lain awake,
envisioning whole trees shearing off at rotten points in their trunks,
branches punching through the roof, flattening him and Carina in the
bed. He imagined them being found out that way.

Carina wasn't home and he sat on her front step. He was preparing
to leave when her car pulled in behind him. She got out and groaned
at the sight of him. 'I've had a bad day,' she said. 'I don't know if I can
handle you right now.'

'Maybe I've come here to profess my undying love.'

She snorted.

They did it with her bent over the small two-burner stove, her skirt up around her waist. In their frantic movements one of them nudged a burner switch and soon the cabin was full of a strange odour. James thought for a moment that he was having some sort of olfactory response to imminent ejaculation. And then Carina was slapping him and swearing. A section of her hair had begun to curl and smoke.

He sat at the foot of the bed facing her. She was on her back inspecting the ends of her hair.

'God,' she said, 'what a day.'

'She's moving her stuff out right now. That's partly why I'm here. I can't really go home for a while. I drove by the house and she was loading boxes.'

Carina didn't say anything. She wet her fingertips in her mouth and rubbed at a burnt end.

'Boxes. Moving, dying, breaking up. All life's great tragedies are marked by the appearance of those goddamn square cardboard units. Such an ominous shade of brown.' He'd thought of this earlier today and it pleased him to say it. He wished she'd come to his side of the bed and put her hand on his leg. He didn't think that was asking too much.

'Fuck,' Carina said. 'I may have to get a haircut to fix this.'

'Part of me didn't actually believe that she was going to leave. We had some serious work-it-out talks. We went camping up on the Stillwater last weekend. We sat side by side next to the campfire. She said the stars above were like a *million diamonds*. She said that. I almost asked her to marry me.'

Carina was pressing her hands to her face. Her fingernails, as always, were immaculate, painted a brilliant red. Each nail was like a little cherry hard candy that James wanted to crush between his teeth.

'I'm serious,' he said. 'I was going to propose. And you know what? Why *can't* the stars above be like a million diamonds? And why, when she said that, did I want to tell you about it immediately?'

James stopped. There was some sort of noise emerging from behind Carina's hands, both of which where now clamped over her mouth. Her fingernails were digging into her cheeks and her eyes were screwed shut. And then she rose from the bed and he could hear her retching in the bathroom.

When she emerged, her dark hair was in beautiful disarray. She was brushing her teeth, one arm crossed over her bare breasts.

Carina had come from San Francisco on a grant to teach creative writing to at-risk girls on the Crow Reservation. She was writing a book about her experiences. For someone who could be so sarcastic, downright caustic, it surprised James to see the level of earnestness with which she approached her job. She loved it. She loved the at-risk girls (a classification that, on the reservation, seemed to encompass the entire population). She approached each class day with happy anticipation. If he happened to entertain the idea of staying over on a school night she would kick him out so she could prepare. She was a teacher and he was a teacher, but what she did was something completely different. He fully acknowledged that. She had a passion. He enjoyed the really nice sense of calm that came from having good health benefits.

She sometimes read him sections of stories or poems, written by her girls. James had to admit that some of the stuff was pretty remarkable. There was one he always remembered, the words themselves and the way Carina had read it, in bed, naked, on her stomach with her feet up in the air, her heels knocking together in time with the words. *I look at him, the boy that doesn't love me, and it's like a badger has climbed into my chest. The badger tramples my stomach while it chews on my heart.*

Carina got into bed. She continued to brush her teeth. She also started to cry.

'I'm sorry,' James said. 'I shouldn't have been talking about all that stuff. It's been tough for me lately and I'm –'

Carina was shaking her head, pointing at the kitchen. 'Can you get me a glass to spit in?' she said, her voice garbled by toothpaste.

When he returned with the glass she spit, handed it to him, and then rolled in bed to face the wall.

'Today, Ellen Realbird went to the bathroom and sawed through her wrists with an obsidian spear-point from the early Clovis era. She asked to be excused and was gone for twenty minutes and I had a weird feeling and I went into the bathroom and there was blood under one of the stall doors and she was in there. James, she was still kind of moving around, slowly, in a pool of her own blood. She was making, like, fish movements or something. Trying to swim through the floor. That will never go away. I will have that forever. And then on the way home I literally caught myself thinking, for a split second, *Damn you, Ellen, you little bitch. Do you have any idea what kind of thing you have just lodged in my brain?* Can you believe that? What kind of person thinks that in response to something like this?'

James was still holding the glass with Carina's toothpaste spit in it. 'Jesus Christ,' he said. 'An obsidian spear-point? The Clovis era?'

'In science class they were having a prehistoric unit. Apparently there was a guest speaker from Montana State who brought visual aids. Ellen pocketed it at some point when no one was looking. Last week I asked them to write me a paragraph about some of their writing goals for the summer. She wrote that she had gotten a job at the Dairy Queen and that she was going to carry a little notebook in her waitress apron so she could just jot down observations about all the interesting people she would see. That's how she put it. She was going to observe and *jot things down*. No one who *jots things down* kills themselves.'

James got into bed and put his arms around her. He'd come to tell her that he was leaving. It seemed rather impossible now – the telling, not the leaving.

In the morning, Carina still sleeping, he pointed the car south. It was green-up, the best time to be driving through the great swathes of western grassland. Crossing Wyoming was like riding a fresh swell of chlorophyll. He pushed his way into Colorado until he hit the front-range traffic on I-25 and then he got a room and ate a bad meal and watched sports highlights before surrendering to the pull of stiff hotel sheets.

He was up early, an egg sandwich and coffee to go. Past Denver the traffic eased and the land flattened. It was still Colorado, but it could have been anywhere. Eventually he broke out and covered the skinny Oklahoma panhandle in about the time it took to listen to an entire Townes Van Zandt album. And then – just as the sun cracked itself down on the vast, oil-pump-studded plain that stretched around as far as he could see – James crossed over into Texas.

His brother lived in a maze of cul-de-sacs and identical two-storey homes with two-car garages. The streets were named after trees or Ivy League colleges. James imagined that if you lined up all the kids and golden retrievers of the neighbourhood on the sidewalk, they too would prove indistinguishable.

Casey's wife, Linda, met him at the door. She was big and brassy and blonde. James had seen her in a bikini once and she had the lone star of Texas tattooed on the small of her back. She pressed a beer into his hand and led him into the study where, predictably, Casey had deigned to remain instead of coming out to meet James. Like Don Corleone, he had always enjoyed *receiving* visitors, especially family members, as opposed to just greeting them, like a normal person.

Casey was sitting at his desk shuffling some papers. He looked up, surprised, as if he hadn't known James was there, as if he hadn't heard him talking to his wife in the kitchen. He stood, they shook hands and then Casey pulled him into an awkward hug, both of them leaning over the expanse of desktop between them.

They hadn't seen each other in almost a year and they launched into all the usual topics – last year's presidential election, the weather as of late, the state of the MSU men's basketball programme, their respective health, their mother's continued descent into Jesus-tinctured battiness.

Linda brought them sandwiches and more beer. When she put the plates down in front of them they each got a smile, a 'there ya go' and a personalized heart-warming Southern term of endearment. He got 'honey' and Casey got 'darlin".

'Damn it, Casey,' James said while Linda was still in earshot, 'why is your wife such a horrible nag.'

'Oh you stop,' she said. 'Y'all are too bad. Y'all holler if you need anything.' And then she went back to the living room to watch TV.

James had read somewhere that a study done of three thousand American couples found that those engaged in traditional gender roles – male breadwinner, female homemaker – were 50 per cent happier than couples who comported themselves less conventionally. He thought about mentioning this to Casey but decided against it. In general his brother was not a man who needed validation that his ways were correct.

Casey got up and closed the door to his study. He poured two glasses of whiskey from a decanter on the sideboard and gave one to James gravely before settling back into his chair. James knew he was loving this. Casey leaned back and sipped his whiskey.

'Well,' he said. 'What's the deal? You having a bit of trouble?'

Casey was a lawyer. One of the most unsatisfying parts of his life, as far as James could tell, was how infrequently his family members needed legal counsel. It was endearing, how ready he was to spring into action, to roll up his sleeves and get litigious to preserve the family honour. 'Going to Billings to get a new muffler put on your car, you say? Well if you get in any trouble over there you call me, understand?' At some point, James realized he might have to get himself incarcerated, just to make Casey feel needed.

'It's not really a legal matter,' he said. 'Affairs of the heart and all that.'

Casey shrugged, disappointed. Somehow most of his whiskey was already gone. 'Hell, I don't know, Casey. I just needed a change of scenery. Do you mind if I loaf around for a little bit?'

'My casa es tu casa, brother, you know that.'

'Gracias amigo. Let's drink more of your fancy whiskey.' James watched Casey pour them both more bourbon, man-sized slugs this time, and he thought that Casey seemed more at home here in his den, with his wrinkle-resistant khakis and his big-haired wife in the next room, than any man had a right to be. If he was anyone other than his brother he might have hated him for it.

They reached across the desk and touched glasses. 'Nice to see you, brother,' Casey said.

'It is,' James said.

Casey leaned back and kicked his feet up on the desk. He wore fleece-lined moccasins.

'Nice slippers.'

'They aren't slippers. They're house shoes.'

'What's the difference?'

'The sole on these is slightly more rugged, I believe. One could feasibly spend a short amount of time out of doors with them. Linda got them for me for Christmas. She's been making baby noises.'

'What do those sound like?'

'"Casey, honey, my ovaries are speaking to you right now. They're parched. They're starting to wither. Are you going to fertilize this garden or what, boy?"'

'She says that?'

'And worse. Much worse. That's the version generally fit for public consumption.'

'You might as well just do it. What's there to wait for? You're rich. You could support a small tribe.'

'A boy wouldn't be too bad. I'd like that actually. But a girl, I don't know if I could take it. And this isn't something I can talk to Linda about very well.'

'What's wrong with having a girl? Girls love their daddies. You wouldn't have to fight with her like you would a boy. Linda would get to have all the awkward talks.'

Casey took a drink of his whiskey and swished it audibly around in his mouth. He swallowed and grimaced. 'One time I was involved with a gal that liked me to put my hand around her throat and squeeze. I mean, she liked me to choke her, James. Now, can you tell me what happens to make a little girl grow up to become a woman who wants something like that?'

James laughed and then he saw that Casey was serious. 'I'm not sure,' he said. 'But, how d'you handle that situation? I mean, did you, you know?' James made a gripping motion with his hand.

Casey shook his head. He drank the rest of his whiskey and set the glass down carefully on a coaster shaped like a bass.

'Shit man, I did more than that. I married her.'

It was mid-June and north Texas was a smoking hotplate. In the cotton fields outside of town farmers were doing something to raise the dust. There was nothing to see and you couldn't see it if there was.

In the late evening James sat on the back porch drinking a beer, half reading a newspaper, sweat dampening the pages. He watched the sun turn red as it sunk through the dust. The houses and roofs and backyards of the neighbourhood were cast in a blood-dusk glow. A Martian suburb awash with the smell of a thousand barbecues being lit.

James finished his beer and finally, mercifully, it was dark. A few degrees cooler, maybe. There were fireflies blinking on and off in the yard. He hadn't seen a firefly in a long time. There were none in Montana as far as he knew. Maybe it was too cold. Years ago he'd been camped next to an old hippie couple in Yellowstone and they'd told him that once, in Iowa, they'd dropped acid and went out and gathered a whole jar of fireflies and then rubbed them all over their naked bodies and then had luminescent sex in a moonlit cornfield. Their obvious happiness at relaying this story gave him a shiver. He saw, in them, all the couples of the world for whom the past held more promise than any potential future. Relationships based largely on reminiscence of things past. Was this what it meant to be rested, content, settled in love? Or, were the old hippies, and all others like them, just wound-up machines running on memories?

A fter a week of loafing at Casey's, the dust and feedlot smell of Amarillo started to wear on him. Casey worked long hours at his office. Being in the house all day with Linda – she did yoga in the living room, she constantly wanted to feed him sandwiches – was making James uncomfortable. The probing questions from Casey at the dinner table made him feel like an underachieving son, stalled out after college, living in his old bedroom.

James found himself a job. An unlikely one at that. It was a ranch-hand position at an outfit outside of Austin, in the hill country. The job description in the classifieds was succinct.

> WANTED: Seasonal ranch labourer.
> No experience necessary.
> Beautiful location. Remote. HARD WORK.
> Fair pay.

James called. He talked to a man who occasionally let out clipped groans, as if he was in pain. Their brief conversation was punctuated several times by loud birdcalls. In less than fifteen minutes he was hired. He had two days before he was to start and he'd forgotten to ask about pay.

When James left Amarillo, Casey shook his hand and wished him luck, as if he were shipping off to basic training. Linda gave him a hairspray-scented hug. 'Y'all take care now darlin',' she said.

He pointed his car south once more into the fiery bowels of the Summertime Republic of Texas.

O utside of Austin the land began to show some contour. The pure flat of the north gave way to wrinkled hills and canyons with cream-coloured limestone walls. He was pleasantly surprised: he'd never known Texas to look like this. He admired the swells of oak-covered ridges, the white caliche ranch roads, glowing under the sun.

Two hours and several wrong turns later he pulled up to a low ranch house tucked under a grove of pecan trees. There was a small pond and a windmill. A red heeler with a grey muzzle came out from under the shade of a parked truck and eyed him without approaching. Peacocks scratched in the gravel, bottle-green feathers resplendent under the sun. James stretched and looked around. His shirt was stuck to his back with sweat.

A man came out of the house. He wore a straw hat and had a cast on one of his legs – ankle to mid-thigh. The leg without a cast was jean-clad and it took James a moment to figure out that the man had taken a pair of his Levi's and cut one leg off three-quarters of the way up. He'd put a double wrap of duct tape around the shortened pant leg to keep it snugged down over the cast. On the foot with the cast the man wore a large rubber galosh. On the uninjured foot he had a cowboy boot. Some folks with a full leg cast in Texas in late June probably just wore shorts. This man was obviously cut from a more rugged cloth.

'You James?'

'Yessir.'

'That's good. I'm Karl. We've talked. Montana, eh?'

'Yes.'

'I been there once. Saw Old Faithful. It could have been worse. Montana's better than a lot of places. But, you know what they say?'

James thought about telling Karl that Old Faithful was actually in Wyoming. He didn't. 'What do they say?'

'In Montana they make cowboys. In Texas they make men.' Karl laughed and wiped at the sweat on his face with his shirtsleeve. 'Montana, I got a broken leg here.' He pointed at the offending member. 'Usually I do everything here myself but, as you can imagine, this has got me limited. How's your back?'

'My back is fine.'

'That's good. We're going to be working. You're going to be working mostly. I'm going to be telling you what to do. There's where you'll bunk. Everything you need should be there.' Karl pointed to a low-ceilinged wing built off the side of the barn. 'Stow your gear and then come on back and I'll give you a tour.'

The bunkhouse was more pleasant than James had expected.

There was a double bed. A small kitchenette. A table with a bouquet of dried flowers. Most importantly, an air conditioner. James cranked it up and tossed his single bag on the bed. The back window looked out over the pond where the heeler was standing up to its belly in the water, panting. James looked in the small fridge. There were two cans of Tecate and a jar of peanut butter. He'd had a refrigerator just like this in his dorm in college. The sight of this one made him indescribably happy.

When James emerged from his room Karl was sitting behind the wheel of an off-road vehicle, kind of like a golf cart, but with large knobby tyres and a camouflaged awning and a rifle rack on the hood. There was a cooler in the back, and as James slid into the passenger seat, Karl reached around and rummaged in the ice, pulling out a beer for both of them. He drank deeply and belched.

'You said on the phone the other day that you're a teacher?'

'Yes.'

'What subject do you teach?'

'Everything, pretty much.'

'What, like kindergarten?'

'No, I actually teach in a one-room schoolhouse. I have around fifteen kids.'

'A one-room schoolhouse? They still have those? Jesus, employment offers weren't exactly flooding your mailbox, or what?'

James laughed. 'It was actually a competitive position. People *want* their kids to go to Pine Creek School. It's selective. We have to turn students down every year. It's a unique learning environment and we consistently get high test scores. We have brochures. That's what they say.'

'I see.' Karl drank and then released the parking brake on the golf cart. 'It's a yuppie one-room schoolhouse, not a real one-room schoolhouse. I'm sure the pay is better. Anyway. It don't matter because your ass is mine for the rest of the summer. Let's get you acquainted with the lay of the land.'

They embarked upon a rambling tour of the 2,000-acre Echo Canyon Ranch, stopping occasionally so Karl could lever himself out of the driver's seat to take a piss. Occasionally deer bolted out in front of them. Once James saw something larger and darker moving off into the brush and then it was gone.

'What happened to your leg?' James asked.

Karl laughed. 'Buffalo fell on me,' he said.

Then the beer cooler ran dry. Karl, reaching and coming up empty, said, 'Well shit.'

Sooner than James would have thought possible they were back in front of the house. 'There you have it, Montana, what d'you think?' Karl said.

James could hear the clank of the windmill turning lazily. The red dog came and put its muzzle on Karl's broken leg. 'It's great,' he said.

'Likely as not you've noticed we haven't got so much as a milk cow on the whole spread.'

'I thought maybe they were in a different pasture or something.'

'Nope. Closest thing we've got is a few buffalo. Nasty things. Stay clear. They'd just as soon gore you as look at you. Same with the elk. Even the females. Especially the females. They'll kick you through a barn door.'

'Elk?'

'Sure. This is a hunting ranch, son. We've got all the exotics. Aoudads, Sitka deer, feral hogs, New Zealand red deer, elk, a few different kinds of antelope. There's things out there that I can't even name off the top of my head. I was driving down to Bandera the other evening and coming up out of the riverbed I saw this animal almost the size of a horse. It had corkscrew-looking horns, spots on the rear half of its body. Now what the hell was that? I have no idea. Who knows where it came from and who knows how long it's been running? All I know is that there's a dentist in Dallas who would pull his own eye teeth to have that thing's head hanging on his wall. That's what we do here. It's what all the ranches around here do. Been that way for a long time and that's why you'll occasionally see a random like that.'

'What do you mean, a random?'

'Just like it sounds. Some animal that was released at one time to be hunted but that just never got killed and was forgotten about or jumped a fence, or whatever. Ranches sell all the time. Fences fall over. Inventory is hard to keep track of. The hill country's full of loose exotics. You've seen the brush. You can't get much more than a few steps off a road and it just swallows you. The African species especially seem to find it just like home.'

James was slightly disappointed. He'd been under the impression that he was going to be out mending fences. Rounding up doggies and slapping hot iron to calves.

'What exactly, then, will I be doing?'

'Oh we'll keep you occupied. At least once a week we have to go around and fill the feeders with shelled corn. That takes a full day. There's over forty of them on the property. Some fences might need shoring up. Some brush might need to be cleared out to keep the shooting lanes open. Like I said, I usually do it all myself but it's just a little bit much right now for this ol' boy.'

James got his own four-wheel-drive golf cart. One of the perks of the job. He filled a gallon jug with water and set out to explore further on his own. Karl said the pain pills he was on were making him woozy and he was going to take a nap.

James started noticing the feeders. They were metal tripods with a hopper operated by some sort of timing device. At a set time each day a measured amount of shelled corn would fall from the hopper to the ground. The feeders were placed in small clearings hacked from the brush. Twenty yards from each feeder, in a lane cut through the trees, was a blind – a small, tin-roofed camouflage-painted shack with low windows from which a rifle could be fired. James went to one of these blinds and opened the door. Inside was an office chair and a pair of ear-protecting headphones.

An office chair – with adjustable lumbar support and rollers and pneumatic suspension system. It was the seat every accountant in the world sat in all day. It seemed strange to think that that same accountant might get a day off and come down here to Echo Canyon Ranch to sit in that same chair some more, listening to the rhythmic clunk of the feeder hopper opening, the musical shower of corn falling to the leaf litter. Waiting with anticipation for something, anything, to present itself for killing.

All the blinds were numbered. The two-track roads were like fairways claimed from the mesquite and shin oak and cedar. James felt that he'd landed on some sort of morbid golf course, where, instead of clubs, the camouflaged hackers toted .30-06s and tallied their day's end score factoring in missed shot bogeys, sand trap woundings, extra clip mulligans – counting pars and birdies and eagles in hides and horns and tusks.

'Fore,' James shouted.

His voice was swallowed immediately by the tangle of dense green that surrounded him. Echo Canyon was kind of a misnomer.

That night his air conditioner melted down. He woke in the early hours, his bed sheet drenched in sweat. There was the god-awful squealing of the hogs rooting in the brush behind the barn. He lay in the dark, thinking about a conversation he'd once had with Carina. She had called him on his lunch break at school to tell him that he didn't value his own profession and this made him unattractive to her.

'You have disdain for those who teach,' she said. 'And yet you do it yourself. That must be exhausting.'

'Why do you say that?'

'Because, when we first met, when you told me you were a teacher, and I said that's great, you said, "You know what they say, those who *can't*, teach." That's a bullshit philosophy. And if you truly feel that way then you should quit teaching immediately before you infect any more students.'

'You called just to tell me this?'

'Yes, I thought you should know.'

James tried to imagine Molly Hanchet, his red-haired sixth-grader, smuggling a scalpel from their dissection unit into the bathroom and opening her veins. He imagined finding her, the red of her blood shaming the red of her hair. He tried to imagine returning to the classroom the next day, all the days after, and it was here that his imagination failed completely. He didn't know much about Carina's childhood but he knew enough to realize that she had once been an at-risk girl. Her resilience and dedication seemed to stem from some deep-seated need to save an earlier version of herself. Could he fairly fault himself for lacking this dimension of commitment? Did one's vocation need to be so deeply personal?

He got up and banged on the A/C with his boot heel. It clanked to life slowly. Out behind the barn there was a vicious cacophony of squealing and grunting and thrashing and then it was silent. Clearly it was going to be a long night, the mind chasing the heart in circles around the moon.

The days passed. True to his word Karl kept James moderately busy. But it was pleasant work, at a stately pace. Lots of golf-cart driving and standing around discussing strategy before anything was actually done. James patched a few fences. He cut and cleared some brush. He filled the feeders, hauling sacks of corn, winching the hoppers down to the ground, smelling that good Midwestern smell as the golden stream poured forth from the tipped bag. On weekend evenings he and Karl would load up in the truck and head to Bandera, the nearest town, for beers and a hamburger. As far as James could tell Bandera was not populated by a single attractive female between the ages of eighteen and forty-five. This relaxed him in a way that he, up until this point, had thought impossible.

He called Casey to update him on ranch life. After listening for a while Casey said, 'Hey, while I got you on the phone I wanted to ask you for something.'

'What?'

'Your life, basically. I want your life.'

'Like, you want to sacrifice me for something, or you need a heart transplant, or?'

'I just want to take off when I want to and go live on a ranch and mend fences and screw around with strange women and drink beer.'

James laughed. 'Don't tempt me brother. I'd take your place in a heartbeat. Wear your house slippers. Drink your fancy whiskey. Enjoy your bank account. Choke your wife.' There was silence on the line for a moment.

Casey cleared his throat. 'Please never mention that again.'

'You're right. Sorry.'

'Seriously though, James. Never change. For the sake of all of us sad bastards who need to live vicariously through you, never stop what you're doing.'

James knew what his brother needed. He gave it to him. He said, 'I have a feeling that all this will be decidedly less thrilling when I'm fifty. You ever think of that? Because I do, all the time. I worry that I'll be doing all the same stuff, just none of it will be quite as good as it used to be. There'll still be strange women but most of the time I won't be able to get it up anyway. I'll still have my freedom but I'll be too tired to go anywhere and I'll probably start to accumulate cats and when I finally ride the big one, sitting alone in my recliner in front of the TV, no one will find me for three weeks and the cats will have eaten most of my face. So there. Stop your bitching. You're living the dream.'

Casey didn't say anything for a few moments. James could hear the rhythmic clicking of a pen.

'You remember Linda's ovaries?'

'How could I forget?'

'Well, we've been walking the tightrope with no safety net for a while. Flying with no parachutes. Rafting with no life jackets.'

'What in the hell are you talking about?'

'We agreed that Linda should go off birth control and just see what happens.'

'And?'

'We're knocked up over here in Amarillo.'

'Oh man, congratulations. Tell Linda I love her. That's great.'

'I still don't know if I'm ready for it all but I guess it's too late. We are about to go shopping for stuff to make one of the spare bedrooms a nursery. Lord help me.'

James could hear the happiness in his brother's voice and felt a small twinge. It stopped short of jealousy. But, just short.

There was a rainy day. A small miracle. The air was thick and humid and it was still hot but the dust laid down. James and Karl pulled the golf carts into the barn and did some maintenance. James had never been mechanically minded and Karl was having a good time exposing his ignorance. 'Hand me that oil-filter wrench there, Montana. No, I said the oil-filter wrench. No, the *oil-filter wrench.*'

'Karl, I don't know what that is.'

'Goddamn son, are you serious? You've never changed your own oil? The decline of a once great nation. Evidence.'

Later, James drove up to the hill where he was able to get spotty cellphone reception. He had one voice message from Carina. 'Call me *immediately.*' This was how she always left him messages. No one else he knew did this and it always drove him to think the worst, that she had been involved in an accident of some kind or that she needed him to bail her out of jail or that she was pregnant. There was something about Carina that placed all of these things firmly in the realm of possibility. But, up until this point it had always been something benign, something like, she had just heard an NPR programme about life on the Wind River Reservation that she thought was horribly off base and she wanted to discuss it with him.

He wasn't sure he was ready to talk to her. He'd called her only once since leaving and he'd kept it vague. He'd told her he was going to visit his brother, and that was it. His life at the ranch was simple, unexamined, not something she'd understand. He could picture the conversation, trying to defend himself in the face of her

incredulousness. *You're filling deer feeders with corn? Are you serious?*
Everything unravelling under her scrutiny. She would accuse him
of trying to hide. 'My god,' she had said to him once. 'Am I the first
adult woman you've ever had to deal with?' They were parked in his
car on the hill overlooking town. This was when they were still stealing
moments wherever they could.

'What is that supposed to mean?'

'Just that you seem incapable of taking anything seriously. Is that
how *she* likes you to be? Or, is it just a coping mechanism you've
developed in order to endure swimming in a pond that shallow?'

'Shallow ponds are the best for swimming. They warm up the
quickest. And you can always touch the bottom if you get tired.'

She looked at him for a long moment. Shook her head. Got out of
his car and into hers.

He figured that she had probably never been swimming in a pond
her whole life. He could see her as a child, in the summer, running
wild through the concrete heat of whatever hellhole she'd grown up
in, the busy city pool her only escape. After that, how could she help
it if her aura was clear blue California chlorine?

He sat for a while watching the rain dapple the truck windshield.
Then he drove back to the bunkhouse and stripped, running
through the rain, to dive in the spring pond. He kicked down until
his outstretched hand felt the muck bottom and then he turned
and drifted slowly back to the surface, opening his eyes to see the
raindrop-pocked roof of water above him. He floated for a while on
his back remembering something Carina had read to him. It was
from one of her girls, part of an essay about swimming in Yellowtail
Reservoir on the Bighorn River.

> When I dive in the water it's like going down
> through Neapolitan ice cream, except, instead of
> chocolate-vanilla-strawberry, it's temperature –
> warm up top and then cool and then cold where
> it's deep and the sun can't reach. That's where

I like it best. I call that the chocolate layer. That's
the flavour my mom tasted when she drove her
car off the high road. Everyone says I look just
like she did at my age.

Often, Carina's life seemed immeasurably more worthy than his.
He checked his level of enthusiasm for the return home. A new
school year at Pine Creek. Anxious parents. Lesson plans. His
classroom had two long bulletin boards that would need to be rehung
with inspirational quotes and motivational posters. These bulletin
boards had become nightmare fodder. In one memorable dream
his posters had somehow morphed overnight so that, on the first
morning of school, the children were greeted by walls plastered with
profanity-laced diatribes and pornographic pictures. He woke up
soon after his firing.

He towelled off and sat at the small table in the bunkhouse. *Call
me immediately.* Maybe he'd write her a letter.

Somehow, it was mid-August. There was more activity on the ranch
than there had been all summer. Housekeepers came to air out
the guest cabins. Men in camouflage shirts with binoculars around
their necks patrolled on golf carts. Hunting season was approaching.
The actual owner of the ranch came from Austin for the day. He was
a big, white-toothed, red-nosed man who didn't have much to say to
James but immediately fell to back-slapping and exchanging barely
coherent Texas good ol' boy insults with Karl. They loaded a cooler
with beer and departed on a golf cart and were gone for the rest of the
day. Apparently he'd made his money mostly in real estate. Probably
a little oil revenue there on the top, like salad dressing.

To James it was fairly clear that men of a certain standing in Texas
needed to own ranches. They needed to have a man like Karl on the
payroll. It's what separated them from the citified businessmen on
the coasts. During the week they might sell and trade commodities
but on the weekends they were ranchers, desperately. How else to

justify their existence, if not by holding themselves to a moral code developed in large part from watching John Wayne movies as boys?

James gassed up his golf cart and took one last long evening drive. The summer was all but spent. He had a six-pack on ice and he drove slowly on his favourite two-track, the brush gathering evening shadow on either side of him until he broke out on the hilltop overlooking the ranch. He was going to watch the sunset and tomorrow he would leave. He was surprised to find that he would miss Echo Canyon. He really would. He hadn't been to town in a week. Hadn't bought anything. Hadn't had lust-filled thoughts toward a strange woman, hadn't had a hangover, or a fast-food meal. It was amazing how these things could accumulate in your system, like toxic heavy metals, without you realizing it.

He drank his beer and watched the deer that were coming out of the trees to the feeder near the hill's summit. He leaned back and propped his feet on the golf cart's dash. A flock of mourning doves came and settled in the grass, close enough that he could hear their chortling love warbles to one another. He noticed the deer at the feeder were looking back over their shoulders to the treeline. And then, a zebra poked its black-and-white-striped head out of the brush and made its way slowly across the clearing as the sun set.

A zebra. It joined the deer at the feeder. The sinking sun burnished its flanks so it glowed like polished variegated copper. The deer were sad dead leaves next to its majesty.

He sat stunned, didn't want to move, but then it was dark and the mosquitoes came out in full force. He turned on the golf cart's headlights and caught the zebra, its eyes like huge white marbles, before it disappeared. He drove slowly back to the bunkhouse, straining for just one more look, but it was gone.

Karl was on his porch scratching the red heeler behind the ears. James pulled up a chair and sat. 'Well,' he said. 'I just saw a random.'

'Yeah?'

'A zebra.'

Karl straightened. 'You're shitting me.'

James shook his head. 'No shit.'

'Huh. I'll be damned. We got a crew of hunters coming in from Fort Worth next weekend. That would be a hell of a way to kick the season off. Those ol' boys would lose their minds over something like that.'

'You'd really let them shoot it?'

'Sure, what the hell else would you do with it?'

'I don't know. Just doesn't seem right.'

Karl shook his head, crushed his empty beer can in his fist. 'I know what you're getting at and you're off base. That thing you saw wasn't a zebra.'

'No. It was a zebra. I'm sure of it.'

'Nope. Zebras are in Africa. That's the only place. A zebra anywhere else in the world ain't a zebra. See what I mean?'

'Not really.'

Karl gave an exasperated sigh. 'You set these Fort Worth boys down in Africa and let them unload on a zebra and then maybe I can see your point. That's not something they're worthy of. But here, in Texas? A Texas man is worthy of anything in Texas. That's how I feel.'

'Karl, I was thinking. What if I stayed on through the fall?'

'What about your one-room schoolhouse and all that?'

James shrugged. 'They'd find a replacement for me quickly enough.'

'What's that supposed to mean?'

'Haven't you ever wanted to be indispensable?'

'Shit. Indispensable don't exist. God's a junk man and he's got spare parts to replace everything he's ever made.'

'What if you have a family, children? My brother's wife is pregnant. No matter what happens, that kid will never have another real father.'

'All sorts of ingrates reproduce. There's nothing sacred about it.'

'I guess,' James said. 'But, I'm serious. If I called and told them I wasn't coming back to teach, would you let me stay on through the fall?'

Karl was using a straightened metal coat hanger to scratch under his cast. 'I'm supposed to get this damn thing cut off in a week,' he said. 'I'm tempted to go get a hacksaw and do the job myself.' He stopped scratching and leaned back. 'Montana, why do you think men come here? The thrill of the hunt and all that? Bullshit. In olden times, when you were sick, you went to the doctor and he vented your blood to release the bad humours. I've seen men cry. Grown men with tears on their cheeks confronting the mangy old buffalo they've just shot. Tears of joy, mind you.' Karl waved his hand as if to encompass the yard, the ranch, Texas as a whole. 'You're here for the same reason as those Fort Worth boys. Even if you try to hide it behind something else. And, I'm going to do you a favour here and tell you what I tell all of them when they get a little drunk on the last day of their vacation and start in about how they want to come down here and buy a little ranch and *just leave it all behind*. Do you know what they say in the bar at closing time?'

'What do they say?'

'You don't have to go home but you can't stay here.'

J ames packed his things and then stretched out on the bed. In a few days he would walk back into his house, his life. It would be stuffy after the summer's vacancy. Her things would be gone – gaping holes in the closets where her clothes had been, the empty place in the toothbrush holder like an unblinking vacant eye. He felt like he deserved a better homecoming. Maybe he'd go to Carina's first. They could sit outside in the grass under the cottonwoods. She would tell him about her summer-school girls and he'd describe Echo Canyon Ranch in ways that made it all seem more spectacular than it really was. He wanted to tell her about the zebra. It was very important that he do it in such a way that she wouldn't dream of laughing.

It was out there, the zebra, somewhere, moving through the sticky darkness. He imagined what the land would look like if you could somehow strip away all the brush – the mesquite and the cedars and the prickly pear and the madroños – to expose the animals. All the randoms. It would be like a goddamn menagerie.

Maybe there was a lion. If there was a zebra then it seemed like anything was possible. He hoped so.

If all was right in the world, there was a lion out there right now stalking the hills, eating deer and hogs to pass the time, but really hunting the zebra. Eventually the two would cross each other in the brush. The zebra would run, gratefully, and the lion would chase, and, ultimately, under the low shade of a live oak, the lion would feast on the zebra's flesh before either one of them had to suffer one more indignity. ■

RIVER SO CLOSE

Melinda Moustakis

She's a good-for-nothing chummer. If she survives a week on the slime line without cutting off her thumb or slicing her wrist, she's hired. And when she's hired she gets paid. 'After you get paid,' says the boss to the new crew, 'we'll ask you what your names are.' Everyone wears slicks and bib overalls and boots, and the only bibs left for her to wear are full of holes. She follows the boss into the main of the cannery and is outnumbered by men with bearded faces. But there are a few women, the older ones sinewy and rough. There are two who look almost as young as she is, blonde hair filling their hairnets, speaking to each other in Russian. Then a woman quickly waves and says, 'I'm Deen.' Deen is about ten years older, is missing a tooth, my dog tooth Deen tells her later, which makes me only half a bitch, don't tell anyone. Deen watches her close and she can feel the watching, an intensity of watchfulness different from all the bearded faces. Deen's watching says, 'Be careful.'

The cannery smells of fish and death and cleaning chemicals and the stink of old refrigerators. There are long metal tables covered in blood. The workers' gloves and bibs are smeared with red and they all stand in a shallow pool of bloody water and guts. The boss explains each job on the line. Headers, he says, work the guillotine, a shovel-shaped blade that comes down and beheads the fish in one swipe.

Heads for soup in Japan. For dog food in the lower 48. Headers pass to bellycutters. Bellycutters ram the end of a knife into the anus of the headless fish and slice up to the neck, ass to belly to throat. Bellycutters pass to slowgutters, who shove their fingers inside the cut and rip out the guts and eggs. Guts to the gut chute. Eggs to the egg chute, where eggers fill buckets and take them to the roe room, where the door must be closed at all times to keep the right temperature, where the roe is washed and inspected. Slowgutters pass to bloodliners, who scrape the spine for the thick black blood. Bloodliners pass to sprayers, who hose all the blood and slime off and pass to frozen or fresh pack.

'Roe,' says the boss, and he holds up a shiny rubied skein of salmon eggs, 'pays for operation. Meat is for profit. Guts go to the gulls. If anything needs saving, you save the eggs first.'

This is her line. She's a bellycutter. And here is her knife. Here is her dead headless fish. Cut ass to belly to throat. Anus to throat. Fish. Knife. Ass to throat.

Her hands are swollen and forget to grasp and close – they ache with cold, with numbness, with a cold past numbness. She watches her fingers and her thumbs so she won't cut them off. Ass to throat. Fish by fish. Piece by piece. Cut a human body that way, and what would happen? Heart, lungs, bowels, stomach – guts spilling out. The brain is the only organ completely caged by bone. Feeling is low, centre, where it is easy to stick a knife.

The men push her ahead in the shower line. 'Chummer here smells like shit. The fresh bait ain't so fresh.' Her eyes close against her body. If she could go without a shower, she would. But there are holes in her bibs and her jeans are soaked with fish slime. The showers are tacked onto the backside of the cannery, as if they were once outdoor showers, but have slanted tin roofs, and are separated by cheap wooden walls. She latches the rickety door and then turns on the water to check the heat. First she takes off her boots, sits on an overturned plastic bucket. Removes her socks and looks down at her ghost-soaked toes – the skin on her feet is mush. Other showers are blasting and the steam is fish and blood and sweat. She tosses off her fleece, then her shirt, her bra. She goes for the button on her jeans. Stops. The wooden walls are breathing, pressing, leaning. She hears knocking on the wall. A man says, 'Baby, I could suck those tits.' And then laughter. She covers her chest with her hands and turns around and huddles under her towel, trembling, and puts her shirt back on. Where is the slat, the hole, the slit? But she needs a shower. She'll wash her clothes while wearing them. She stands under the spout of water, fully dressed. Runs the bar of soap quickly over her hair. The slick of slime on her jeans doesn't dissolve in the suds. The water will never be hot enough.

Soaking wet and half clean and shivering she walks to her car that she's been living in and ignores the stares and whistles. She drives out of camp, fast, so they won't see her cry. She finds a place to park and sleep, some turn off the highway, some unmarked road. Wrings out her clothes and lays them over the seats. Cracks a window. Sets the alarm for five. Dead fish smell in the shower. Dead fish in the drain. Dead fish on her skin. Dead fish under her fingernails, in her hair, in her car.

She can't sleep. The sky doesn't sleep either – the midnight sun a wide-awake eye. And her hands do not sleep. Her hands do not dream. They are holding a fish, holding a knife, cutting and slicing in one long line.

Her clothes don't dry during the night. She has a choice, cold wet jeans or ruin her only other pair. Wet jeans, for now. She'll change into shorts and put bibs over them in one of the outhouses at the cannery.

When she opens the outhouse door with bibs on and the jeans over her shoulder, Deen is waiting, arms crossed. 'So, you're from California,' she says, with her eyes narrowed in disapproval. She would have seen the car's licence plates.

'I'm from all over.'

'So's everyone else,' says Deen. 'What part of California?'

'The armpit.'

Deen nods and uncrosses her arms. 'If you ever have to use those filthy showers here again,' she says. 'Let me know. I've got a bottle of cheap-ass vodka. Can't drink the stuff, but it might wash that grease out of your hair.' Deen's curly hair is shoved up into a stocking cap. She usually bathes in the river, in the glacial water. Her own spot, and she's not telling where. 'But you can go to the Tesoro gas station a few miles away and get a real shower with hot water, three dollars for ten minutes,' she tells her. 'You know the whole camp is calling you Suds,' she says. 'Squeaky clean.'

The camp is a cluster of cars and vans and trailers, or, at your own risk, a tent, where workers sleep near the cannery. Joey, a header who drove in from Oregon, stays in a tent in the back of a truck. At least, he says, he'll have a warning when a bear shows up. We're all walking bear bait, he says and shoves beef jerky in his mouth while he heads out to take a leak in the woods. No one uses the outhouses unless they have to. The cannery toilets are rusted out and waiting for repairs.

The job is sixteen hours on, eight hours off. Eight minus overtime usually means six. Six hours to eat, sleep, piss. The trick is not to combine any of these, Deen tells her. But it happens. Fall asleep pissing. Fall asleep in a bowl full of oatmeal. If you piss in your sleep, you won't smell any worse than the bangers drinking through their six hours off. Fall where you need to fall. Fall asleep fucking if you have to. As long as you're not on the line, near a blade, or a knife.

A new hire, a rookie, arrives the next day, a fresh-faced college kid who smells like toothpaste. 'Just what we need,' says Deen. 'A frat boy. I give him one day, tops.'

'I give him two days,' says Joey, on his smoke break. He has already given away four of his hand-rolled cigarettes.

'Willing to bet money?' says Deen.

'I'll bet a bottle of Jip,' says Joey.

The rookie ends up across from her as a bellycutter. He's

a whistler and a high-fiver. Two people tell him to shut the hell up. Three hours later, the rookie's knife goes into his glove, the blood sprays, the thumb hangs by a small shred of bone and skin.

'Stop screaming,' Deen tells him. 'We got to get you on ice.'

The rookie tries to run, flail, flee. The thumb flaps and spurts blood on the wall, on bibs, on Deen's face as she tries to corral him. He's a wounded animal full of panic. He knocks over Joey and the two Russians.

'Punch his lights out,' Deen yells at her. He's coming toward her but her hands are numb and she doesn't move. Joey runs up and takes a bare-knuckled swing. The crack means more blood, means the rookie has a broken nose, and Deen says, 'Holy fucking shit,' but at least he's knocked out and still. They stick his fist in a box of ice and drag him to Suds's car and shove him in the front seat and Deen drives him to the hospital in Soldotna. When Deen returns a few hours later, she is alone. The cannery is still shut down for bleach and clean-up. Suds tries to scrub the bloodstains off the seat and Deen says, 'Good luck with that. I told the doctor what happened. He looked at the poor kid and said, "Welcome to motherfucking Alaska," and laughed his face off.'

The rookie doesn't know how lucky he is. A sharp blade is a sharp blade. The stitches will heal and he'll sleep at night. She'd give anything to have that kind of sleep.

The fish count the days and the days count the fish. Count the fish by slice by cut by edge. Count pay and lost pay and docked pay and stashed pay and overtime. The cannery counts in pounds. One hundred thousand pounds a day. River so close but she can't hear it over the belt and crank of the slime line. Or the shrieks of gulls picking through the fish-gut pile.

The line closes for clean-up and to hold a mop or broom or spray nozzle or bottle of bleach, to use a different muscle, a different rhythm, feels like a miracle. Wash the belt, the knives, the table, Thank you, I will, she says. Please, can I sweep the water-thinned blood and guts to the drain? Baptize the floors in bleach, breathe in the chemical air that isn't fish.

There is a bloodliner named Marcus, with a goat beard that covers up the sharp angles of his pretty-boy face. During clean-up he finds a decapitated king salmon head, sticks it on his hand and puppets. The fish mouth moves to made-up jingles of 'Day of the Spawn' and 'You Fillet Me' and 'What's Glove Got to Do with It?'. The blonde Russians smile and take turns pulling at his beard. Or they try to take away the faded blue baseball cap he wears backwards, SWEDEN stitched in yellow letters. Those are the better days. The lighter days. Now-and-then days King the puppet says, in a low gravel, 'Why are you here?'

'Get that fish out of my face,' says a header.

'It beats jail,' someone else says.

'You sure about that?' says King. Then he turns to her for the first time. She can almost feel the wet on her skin and leans her neck away from the fish head that looms close to her ear.

She clenches her jaw and stands very still.

'You got to be careful,' he says, even closer, and his beard almost bristles her skin. 'Dead girls, they're everywhere.'

Cut a woman ass to belly to mouth, and connect all the holes and what you have is meat. In this world, she is either meat or knife. Or meat that carries a knife, that sleeps with one under a pillow, grip ready at the switch. You asked for it, dead girl.

The shift ends early and the sun has been out all day.

'We're going to go for a swim,' says Deen. 'Forget the gas station shower and wherever you go off to,' she says. 'Stay in the trailer with me and the Russians.'

'No,' she says to Deen.

'You know how to swim, don't you?'

'I'm a fish.'

'Well then, let's see if you can drink like one,' Deen says. 'Joey's got some Jips and a fresh bag of ice.'

'I'm not sleeping here,' she says.

'You're a pain in the ass,' Deen says.

She and the Russians follow Deen, who carries a pistol for bears, through the thin patch of woods behind the cannery that leads to the river.

'Suds, you got a gun, right?' says Deen. 'You don't you can borrow one of mine.'

'I got a knife,' she says.

'Only idiots don't have guns out here, you know that. A bear gets you and they'll say good riddance,' says Deen.

'That's fine.'

'It won't be fine when a bear is attacking you. You know what they go for first? The hands. Then the face.'

Deen leads them downriver, out of sight of the cannery and the men. The glacial water is a bright turquoise colour unlike any she's seen and it's so cold it burns. Deen and the Russians rush right in and she gasps when she tries to follow. She's the only one not naked.

'Come on,' says Deen.

She convinces herself and steps in up to her knees, where the water is still clear. The river bottom is sharp and uneven with rocks and she leans down to pick up a few from under her feet. But in her hands the rocks are smooth and glossy, speckled green and grey and brown. One is stuck with the point of an old, broken-off fish hook.

'Stop looking and start swimming,' shouts Deen. Suds tosses the rocks into the water. Ahead of her, there's a drop-off where the river becomes cloudy and deep and there are shadows, smears that must be salmon running up. Or filleted salmon carcasses floating down. Rotting flesh. Fishing line. Old hooks. She turns back to shore. She'll tell them the water was too cold – that she's used to heat and dust and desert. She dries off her feet and puts her boots back on. Deen has left the gun sitting on a towel near the bank. The clouds creep in and the water's reflection turns into a slick of grey. One of the Russians named Svetlana starts a splashing war and then Deen swims away from the splashing and walks up the cut. 'I could teach you to shoot,' she says, and she bends down for the towel, arm pressed against her large breasts.

'I know how to shoot.'

Deen laughs. 'Like you know how to swim? You know how to shoot the breeze, and that's about it.'

I f only she could take down the sun, the midnight sun, and lie in the dark and not be afraid. In her car, in the back seat in a sleeping bag, with a knife within reach, with an empty coffee can so she doesn't have to go out near the river to piss, she covers her face with an old driving map. Where is the darkest place, where no light can come in? Some days it is in the belly of a fish. The ink eye of a king. A knife point beyond skin.

K ing the puppet is a new fish head every night. Glassy dead eyes, fixed. And she never knows how Marcus will change his voice. Tonight King has a string of guts hanging from his fish mouth.

King lunges at Svetlana. 'Is there something in my teeth?' he asks, high and shrill.

Svetlana slaps King across the silvered cheek. 'Away,' she says.

'You've got no guts,' King says.

'Away,' she says again.

King moves on to Joey, who is spraying off the knives.

'Are you you?' says King.

'Man, what does that even mean? Why can't you tell a joke or something?'

'You know what they say about men in Alaska?' says King.

'The odds are good but the goods are odd,' says Joey. 'Everyone knows that.'

'So what do they say about women in Alaska?'

'Good for a limited time only?' says Joey.

'They're the last resort in the last frontier,' King says too loud. 'That, and one is too many.'

Marcus turns in Suds's direction, catches her watching him. With King's head, he draws an H in the air. Then an I. He waves with his other hand. She almost acknowledges him but looks away and starts stacking the empty crates.

Sleep or shower? She knows she smells like fish, but she can't smell it any more. The others won't care that she smells, is what she tells herself. The fish don't care that she smells like fish. But the cranky gas station attendant, with his big belly zipped up in tan coveralls, cares. Whenever she walks in, he wrinkles his nose and says, 'You fucking stink.'

Usually, she ignores him. 'You're a fucking jerk,' she says this time.

'Look who's alive,' he says. 'I've met rotting moose carcasses that smell better than you.'

'I've seen rotting moose carcasses that look better than you.'

He thinks this is funny and slaps the counter near an I'D RATHER BE FISHING sticker. 'But anyone could smell you way before they'd ever see me.'

She holds out the cash. 'Shower.' She notices that someone has crossed out the word 'fish' on the sticker so it now reads I'D RATHER BE FUCKING.

'You got another ten minutes for free,' says the attendant. 'I'm trying to make the world a better place.'

'It would be better if you weren't in it,' she says.

'You like cold water, don't you?'

She checks the walls of the shower for cracks and peepholes, like every time. She should have kept quiet, not made herself loud and visible. But like every night, the water is scalding.

She's drying the knives when King appears over her shoulder, close to her jaw. She feels the cold and wet and tries to shake him off. 'I have something to tell you,' he says, quiet. She notices Deen watching.

'Keep it to yourself,' she says to King.

'Keep it to yourself yourself,' King says.

'I'll keep it if it's worth keeping.'

Kings turns and now she is eye to dead-fish eye. 'The square of the circle is the circle squared,' he says. 'And your circle needs to be squared.'

She looks up at Marcus. There are grey and golden flecks in his hazel eyes. 'What circle is that, exactly?' she says, with a hint of a smile.

'Some would call it the Arctic Circle.'

'What?' she mouths.

'I didn't mean –'

'The fuck you did,' she says, and backs away.

Now she and Marcus have attention. Marcus shrugs off the glares and King opens his mouth and gasps and hurries away, looking over Marcus's shoulder.

She sweeps the pink run-off toward the drain in the floor.

'Is he bothering you?' says Deen. 'You can tell him to knock it off, you know.'

'I know.'

'Knowing and doing are two different things,' says Deen. 'But here's some advice, fuck one and they'll think you want to fuck them all.'

Some nights the stars are fish scales. Some nights the stars are bullet holes. Awake. Dead. Her hands keep under the sun, cutting through sleep, cutting into sleep, cutting her out of sleep. She will cut them off. Lay them on the front seat of the car to dry. Reattach them in the morning. This night the stars are stones in a dark river. This night the stars are eyes.

They all need the money, except for Marcus. Rumour is he's floating on family money after flunking out of law school and his dad knows the owner. There's a group of workers, all ex-cons, who are going in on a car repair shop, but they like to play poker. So they make bets in fish hearts and fish eyes and fins. What is already dead can't kill their plan. One Wednesday Marcus joins their game for the first time. Thursday the line is moving too slow and Marcus throws a fish head and then there's a swarm at the cannery that funnels outside. No knives, just fists. One of the ex-cons ends up with a broken nose. The other with a broken finger. Marcus has a black eye. All three finish out their shifts and no one agrees on how the fight started. That night Deen collects swim bladders from the gut pile and washes them clean. In the morning, she shows up with a bucket of the swim bladders blown up and tied off like balloons. She grabs a screwdriver and a hammer and goes into the broken bathroom and brings out a rust-stained toilet seat, pours vodka on it and her hands, nails it to a piece of wood and nails the wood to an outside wall. She throws one of the finger-length bladders at the toilet seat and it bounces off the rim, but doesn't pop when it lands on the gravel. 'Shoot some hoops and get some of that hot air out of your heads,' she says. The next day, a repairman shows up to fix the bathroom.

Svetlana finds Marcus splayed out on the floor near an empty egg cart.

'Funny very,' she says, without a bit of humour. He has pink foamy spit coming out of his mouth, fish guts spilling out of a hole in his bibs near his stomach. Everyone saw him stage the scene.

'Gout,' Svetlana yells. 'Gout,' and she means 'get out' and maybe she means 'you have a disease'.

It happens. No one calls her chummer, rookie or piece of shit. She is one of them. She smells like them. Her hair is grease. Her bones are flesh and her flesh is bone. This isn't her life. She's waiting for the real one. The one where she has a bed again. The one that is always out there, after the cannery job, after she saves up enough money.

'What's your story?' says Deen. 'Good girl runs away for a summer?'

'There's nothing to tell,' she says. Before she left home two years ago, her mother said, 'I told you not to fuck up like I did, and now I hate you for not fucking up.' She doesn't have a story because everyone else has one, has too many of them.

'I like you,' says Deen. 'I shouldn't, but I do. I know you stash all of your pay in your car and I think of how easy it would be, to steal your car and all that money and then I'd be that much closer to buying a boat and a licence. I wouldn't even feel guilty about it, not for a long-ass while. But, you know, that's just asking the fishing gods for bad luck.'

'I had a dream that I set your hair on fire,' she says. Which isn't true.

'That doesn't make us even,' says Deen. 'You'd have to actually do it. But you better put your money somewhere else.'

'And how do you know I didn't steal this car?'

'Suds,' she says. 'You don't have it in you.'

What is in her? What is in her that anybody would ever want? A salmon heart is a dark black red. A clump of slick mud. A seed of blood. Her sleep is red and silver. The silver of cleaned knives and metal tables, the silver of slabs of fish, of fish heads, eyes still with shock, mouths cocked open.

She wakes up in a gasp. Where is she and why is the car shaking? There's an animal the size of a refrigerator outside the front windshield. A bear is slamming the hood of the car with his two front paws. She climbs into the front seat and honks the horn. The bear stands his ground. In the early haze, his face is a moon of brown with dark tips for ears and lighter fur on his snout. Then she hears a loud grunt and there's another bear, black nose pressed to the cracked-open window right behind her, claw scraping at the glass. Keys, where are the keys, and she cranks the ignition. She doesn't have time to reverse and turn around so she wrenches the steering wheel to the right and slams the gas and spins gravel. The car lunges when the tyres find traction and there's another scrape, then a thud as the corner of the hood clips the first bear in the stomach, and he growls and runs off. She speeds away, catches the other bear in the rear-view mirror as it watches her leave. She drives the bumpy road for a few miles, until she finds a clearing to turn around. She has to go the way she came, over the same knuckle, to get to the highway. Punch the gas – if there's a bear she'll hit it. They both could die. In the blur of woods and the long yawn of morning, she braces for a collision, hands clamped to the steering wheel, not breathing. But the bears are gone. She makes it to the highway. Then parks at the Tesoro.

The front bumper is hanging off. There are claw scratches and paw dents on the hood and the side. The car is not stolen, not yet. Borrowed, was how she put it to herself. Her room-mate won't be back until the end of the summer.

A cold slimy thing touches her ear and she starts.

'Did something eat your car?' says King. His voice is a rasp.

'I don't have time to talk,' she says.

'What are you afraid of?' says King.

'What are you afraid of?' she says. She wipes her ear with her sleeve.

'Fishermen, obviously,' says King. 'And hooks and nets.' King's voice becomes gruff. 'You didn't answer my question.'

'What are you most afraid of? Marcus?' She puts her hand over King's fish mouth. She waits for a clever line of bullshit.

Marcus puts the fish head down on the table near a row of bloodied knives. 'People,' he says and his eyes widen. And he's still talking in King's voice. 'People are the scariest thing.'

She nods. 'People will eat you.'

'People –' He stops and switches to his own voice, peers into her face. 'People will tear you to pieces,' he says.

'People will what people will,' she says. She stares back at him.

He reaches out and hooks a finger under the shoulder strap of her bibs. 'I'd let you tear me to pieces,' he says.

A thrill runs up her neck. 'Let me?' she says.

'Just you, Suds,' he says, and gives the strap a small tug and releases it. 'Don't tell anyone.' His hand moves up to touch a few wisps of her hair.

Her face reddens. 'I bet you say that to all the girls,' she says.

'I don't bet on girls,' he says, and glances beyond her. Then he turns abruptly to the table and picks up King the fish head. Svetlana has come out of the roe room and is walking slowly, sneaking toward Marcus. She motions for Suds to keep quiet by putting a finger to her lips. Svetlana snatches the bill of his backwards cap and runs away and he chases after her with King.

'Cut that shit out,' says Joey.

Hands for cutting. Hands for a knife. Hands for touching. Hands to touch. She can't sleep and drives and parks somewhere else and can't sleep and drives again. She parks the car on a pull-out on the highway, where there is an overlook. The river is below, a liquid jewel, the blue and green of it a shock, bright and running.

She drinks more coffee than usual and prays for a buzz to carry her through the day. At the close of the shift she trudges, out of tiredness and habit, to the outhouses, even though the toilets have been fixed. She opens one outhouse door, and finds Marcus bare-ass, Marcus fucking Svetlana, Svetlana bent over, he has one hand over her eyes and the other over her mouth. Marcus turns his head to the side, still wearing his SWEDEN baseball cap, and smiles at her. She slams the door shut and walks toward the cannery and the newly repaired bathrooms.

During clean-up, she sweeps the bloody water around the outskirts of the tables to the drain, away from Svetlana, and far away from Marcus. Marcus drapes a pair of bib overalls over his arm so that King the fish head now has floppy legs and King starts singing 'You've Got Me Under Your Skin'. Finally, someone says, 'Get to work, fish face.' Marcus, with his free hand, grabs a sprayer and starts spraying and keeps singing until one of the ex-cons knocks the fish head off of his hand. Marcus raises the sprayer toward the ceiling and announces, 'Man down. Man down.' Then Joey grabs the sprayer and tells him, 'Quit it. We've put up with this all summer. Now let's get this done so we can get some sleep.' Two ex-cons glare at Marcus until he grabs the sprayer back and gets to work on the blood-splattered table and everyone else returns to their jobs.

Marcus appears in front of her with a broom, blocking her path. 'Seems you saw a little show today, Suds,' he says and winks.

She sweeps faster, past him, and heads to the drain.

'I should sell tickets,' he says to her back.

'I'm not buying,' she says.

There's a line no one can cross. That she won't cross. And nothing will happen to her. She won't happen. She needs a line that stretches out, forward, and doesn't double back into a knot.

In this line no one loves her or knows her. And that is a relief. No one loves her or knows her. That is a loneliness.

They all pull three hours of overtime when the cannery is slammed with a salmon run and she decides not to shower at the gas station, not to drive around looking for another place to sleep, and instead to stay at camp for the first time. She parks in front of Deen's trailer and Deen tries to make her sleep inside, but she knows there's no room.

'Suit your goddamn self,' says Deen.

Bottles and cans of beer are opened. Low talk of how feet are killing, backs are aching. Then camp settles in for the night and she feels the pull of rest. Keeps a knife close.

'Suds,' she thinks she hears through the barely open window. She shakes it off. And then a voice sings, high, 'Suuudsy.'

She opens her eyes to a big eye peering in the window.

The knife flies out of her hand and hits the inside of the car door before she realizes it's a big fish eye in a big fish head.

'That wasn't very nice,' mouths the fish, sharp. 'It's just King,' and the voice drops down with the name.

'Marcus, go away,' she says. She's shaking. She makes sure the door locks are secure. The knife is somewhere under the front seats.

'Let me in,' says King. 'I just want to talk.' His slimy cheek presses into the pane.

'I'm sleeping,' she says. 'You should be sleeping too.'

Another shiny fish head, dusted with dirt, pops up. 'We're not tired,' both fish mouths say. Then a little louder, 'Let us in.'

She could reach toward the front seat and honk the horn. Yell and wake up the whole camp.

'What's she so afraid of?' says one King to the other.

'Marcus, if you want to talk, then talk,' she says.

'You're going to unlock the door and let us in,' say the Kings. 'That's how it works.' The fish heads drop from view.

Marcus appears, clean-shaven and smooth. He's not wearing his baseball cap. His hair, wild and thick, makes his face seem boyish and fragile. 'Besides, what good is talking,' he says in his own voice, 'when there are so many other things we could do?' The slug of his tongue licks the glass.

She doesn't move. She doesn't say anything. He stares at her and she stares at the long streak his tongue leaves on the window.

'Sorry,' he says. He wipes the streak with his sleeve. Presses his forehead to the glass and winces. 'I'm sorry. I'm a fucking idiot.' He leans down and comes up with one of the King fish heads. 'Can we come in now? We're sorry, aren't we?' and King nods. 'He's sorry,' says King.

'You can't,' she says.

'I'll leave the fish heads outside.' Marcus disappears and then raises only his hands, as if surrendering. 'I'm all yours.' His smile cuts his face in half. 'I've always been yours.'

'Not always,' she says.

'I just want to say goodbye,' he says. 'I'm pretty sure I'm getting fired tomorrow.'

She can't stop looking at the sharp angles of his clean-shaven jaw. How much younger he is, and newer. She unzips the sleeping bag and slides across the back seat toward the door. Puts her hand on the handle. Decides to roll down the window instead.

'That's all I get?' he says.

'That's all you deserve.' She places her left hand over the pull-up lock. And the other she tucks under her leg.

He rests his elbows on the sill. 'You ever had beef jerky in Albuquerque?'

'You ever had –' She shakes her head. 'That's not fair.'

'You're not fair,' he says. He strokes his chin as if he still has a beard. 'Notice anything different?' He raises his eyebrows.

Her hands want to touch the soft hollow of his cheek.

'Jesus, I'm gone.' He exhales. 'I'm so gone.' His eyes slick with tears.

'You're here,' she says.

'Am I?'

Both of her hands raise up, her fingertips graze the sides of his face.

'You ever been so gone,' he whispers, moving in, 'you'd fuck a fish?' Before she can answer he grabs the back of her head and puts his mouth on hers. He's pressing too hard and she can't breathe. There's something strange in his mouth, a small soft ball, and now it is in her mouth, and she's choking and grasping for a hold to pull away, at his hair, his shirt. Is he going to unlock the door? Yank her out of the car? The knife is lost under the seats. She can't scream. She claws and kicks. Sets her teeth against his. Then a sound somewhere, a hinge and a slam. He lets go and runs off. She spits and sucks in air and there on the seat is a fish eye, cold black at the centre. Her whole body gags. She throws the eye out of the window and scrambles into the front seat and drives to the gas station, sick. She doesn't have any of Deen's vodka in her trunk, but she has water and a bar of soap and she washes out her mouth. Washes her face. Finds the knife. Locks the doors twice.

There's a pounding and she wakes with a sudden, frantic reach to make sure the car doors are locked, a frantic reach for the knife. She realizes she is in the driver's seat. Somehow she dozed off. Her heart pulses. The windows are fogged up. She recognizes the gas station attendant's voice and blots out a spot on the glass to make sure it is him. She rolls down the window a few inches.

'It's six thirty,' he says. 'Wild night? What happened to your car?'

'I had to leave somewhere fast,' she says, relieved it is him. She has never slept at the gas station before, or in the front seat.

'I don't want any trouble.'

'I'm late,' she says. She presses her groggy face against the cold of the window.

'You're not supposed to sleep here,' he says.

'You're not supposed to care,' she says.

'Have I told you today you still smell like shit?'

She doesn't have time to take a shower and she can't afford to lose a day. She arrives at the cannery, bracing to see Marcus, wondering how to explain what happened last night to Deen. But Joey rushes up to tell her Svetlana found the word 'Suds' spelled out on the floor near the roe room with skeins of drying, gummy salmon eggs. She started throwing what she could reach, knives and gloves and bins. She was yelling in Russian and the most anyone could make out was Marcus's name and no one could find him. The boss went berserk and threatened to fire everyone over the wasted eggs and ordered the mess to be scraped up, was going to dock everyone's pay until Deen told him it was all because of Marcus. 'We told Svetlana to take a breather,' Joey says.

On break, the crew heads outside to smoke and then Suds sees Svetlana who sees her and points and shouts. Deen drags Svetlana, punching and flailing, back to the trailer.

'You weren't – you and Marcus? Where d'you go last night? Is that why you were late?' asks Deen.

Her mouth, even after coffee, still tastes like a bar of soap. This is her chance to tell Deen. She says, 'Too many people so I drove to the gas station. Forgot to set my alarm.'

'No one really knows Marcus's deal,' says Deen. 'Saw him here the last two summers. Hitch-hikes in. Hitch-hikes out. He'll be back, unless he ends up in a ditch.'

'Wasn't he fired?' she says.

'He never gets fired.'

'He took her money, didn't he?'

'Even worse,' says Deen. 'He didn't take nothing.'

S he sleeps in a different spot each night. Or tries to sleep. Leaves the windows up. She can't see out. And nothing can see in. There is no sky. There are no woods. No river. No animals. There is the fog of her breathing. And her.

T wo weeks left in the season and a record salmon run hits hard and spikes. Red fever. Fish frenzy. Svetlana returns to the roe room after two days and there is no time to think about Marcus. If he walked through the door, everyone would welcome the help. If a bear walked through the door, she would hold out her calloused hands and let it bite off every one of her fingers to the bloody stump. She feels a hand clasp her right wrist and she jerks, but the clasp steadies her knife. She has fallen asleep standing up and the slowgutter next to her is waking her up.

'Don't fuck up,' he says.

To stay alert, she says it over and over to herself. When the shift ends, the guts around the drain have piled up into a mound and Joey has to shovel it to the trash. Someone says, 'I'm going to take a long bitchass shower in bleach, I swear.'

N erves and muscles twitch. Stand, they twitch, when she rests. Rest, they twitch, when she stands. Sleeping is more work than working. To sleep is to unlearn. Uncut every cut. Unknife every knife. Unline every line. Unmouth every mouth. But not everything can be undone.

A fter the last night of clean-up there is a big bonfire to celebrate. Jugs and bottles and cans are put in buckets filled with ice from the cannery.

'Didn't think you'd survive the season, Suds,' says Deen. 'But you did. Now I owe Joey fifty bucks.'

'You better pay up,' says Joey. He's sitting on a cut tree stump.

'How about I give you that toilet-seat basketball hoop instead?' says Deen.

'I'm not that drunk,' says Joey. 'Don't worry, Suds, we didn't have a bet. And if we did, Deen wouldn't have bet against you.'

'I'm not so sure,' says Suds. The borrowed car has also survived, but there's still the rookie's bloodstains on the seat and floor, bear scratches and dents on the hood – and even after all the rain and dirt, she knows where Marcus left his mark on the window.

The smoke thickens with the burning of sweat-stained and fish-slimed shirts and pants and socks. Deen flares up the coals by spitting booze through the gap of her missing tooth in a long, arching stream. Svetlana, drunk and singing, sits on Joey's lap. One of the ex-cons stands up and tells a story about the one and only time he ran away from the cops and didn't get caught, his arms raised, the tall flames behind him. From where Suds is listening, the shadows of his hands are mouths trying to eat fire. And in this light, in this life, no one loves her or knows her. Not yet. ■

CHRIS ADRIAN · AYANA MATHIS · JACKSON TAYLOR · DANYEL SMITH · JUSTIN TORRES · TAYLOR PLIMPTON

THE WRITER'S FOUNDRY MFA

to be, not to seem.

Tim Bebeau (top) fights Keegan Osborn (bottom)
Northern Lights Casino, Walker, Minnesota, March 2012

THE FIGHTERS

David Treuer

'People treat you differently when you lose and when you win. Obviously they treat you better when you win.'
– Mark Coleman, former UFC Heavyweight Champion

I. What I saw on 17 March 2012 at the Northern Lights Casino on Leech Lake Reservation

I saw many things. I saw Josh Maudrie fight Josh Alder while his coach yelled 'DO YOUR JOB DO YOUR JOB!' and he did and afterwards he said, almost in tears, 'I did it Coach. I did it. I did my job.' I saw Tim Bebeau fight Keegan Osborn while his coach (same coach from Brainerd) yelled 'DO YOUR JOB! DO YOUR JOB!' and he didn't. I saw Tori Nelson defeat my cousin Tony Tibbetts after throwing a dozen illegal elbows, enough so Tony couldn't breathe after the second round. I saw a lot of Indian fighters – Tony Tibbetts and Nate Seelye and Tim Bebeau and Josh Thomson and Dave Smith. I saw some of them win and some of them lose. I saw, for the first time, Indians beating up white people in front of a sold-out crowd and I heard the crowd roar. I saw a 47-year-old fighter from the reservation town of Ball Club whose gym was called the Den of Raging Mayhem beat my unbeatable cousin Nate Seelye. (Another fighter was introduced as fighting for 'Team Crazy'.) I was told to give a big round of applause to the King of the Cage Ring Girl and *Maxim* 'Hometown Hottie' Shannon Ihrke from Walker, Minnesota, and I did. I saw fighters with nicknames like 'Timberwolf' and 'High Definition'. I saw a sold-out crowd in our reservation casino, and while my nephew Caleb tuned out the fights and tuned in Skrillex on his iPod while my mother checked her watch to see if she was missing *Law & Order*, I saw two, maybe three, ex-girlfriends, and my cousins Josh, Jason, Delbert, Tammie and Amber, and my uncles Jerry, Davey and Lanny. I saw a sea of baseball caps and braids and Indians and whites. I saw the good people of Leech Lake and Walker get up and cheer and I with them as we watched the fighters – many of them unprepared but willing, all of them brave – step into the cage and fight.

As I watched the fighters and watched the crowd it was clear we couldn't be further from the Ultimate Fighting Championship – UFC – the premier mixed martial arts league. There were no big sponsors, no scouts, no pre-publicity. We were in the middle of a reservation in northern Minnesota and everyone had a day job, or needed one. Instead of the glamour of the UFC we had home-town boys (and girls) who brought out the pleasure of speculation as much as that of spectacle: How would I do in there? Could I do it? Could you? It was easy to feel that little if anything separated us from those in the cage except the willingness to be there. This was like the wrestling matches of old where the promoters mixed local talent with professionals and everyone had a role to play: the up-and-comer, the dandy, the rascal, the working man, the prodigy, the returning hero, the snake, the All-American. There were all the body types, too: the farm boy, the athlete, the wrestler, fat, thin, used up, tattooed with what can only be called bad penmanship. Roland Barthes might as well have been writing about mixed martial arts on the Leech Lake Reservation when he said that many might think wrestling 'an ignoble sport. Wrestling is not a sport, it is a spectacle, and it is no more ignoble to attend a wrestled performance of Suffering than a performance of the sorrows of Arnolphe or Andromaque'. On the reservation there are plenty of reasons why a man might step into the cage, and plenty of reasons why the fights are so electrifying: those reasons derive from our history and from our suffering. Contrary to what Barthes suggests, motives and consequences are not abolished. They are the lifeblood of the fight. But something, surely, other than the chain link, must separate the spectators from the combatants. Something, too, must separate the reservation from everything around it, other than just our blood.

Oh, I saw a lot in Walker, Minnesota, at the Northern Lights Casino in March 2012. What I didn't see was what I had come there to witness: the Main Event. My cousin Sam Cleveland was supposed to fight his last professional fight. But he didn't.

II. What happened to Sam?

What didn't? Sam was thirty-eight, on the far side of fighting age but not over it yet, not by a long shot. 'I still got a lot of power, still got a six-pack – how many other 38-year-olds around here can you say that about?' he said when I talked to him a month before the fight. He was scheduled to fight the Main Event in the King of the Cage 'Winter Warriors Showdown' and had gone from 175 pounds to 161 in three weeks of dieting and running. His body looked hard and lean. His face showed the strain – that and not a few scars from years of fighting. He might have had the body of a thirty-year-old, but he had the face of a fighter who has taken his share of abuse.

Sammy is my first cousin. Like me he grew up at Leech Lake, but, as he put it, much more 'in the mix'. Like me, he had suffered a particular kind of racism as a red-haired, fair-skinned Indian on the rez. Which is to say no one ever let him forget what he was or what he wasn't. But he weathered it well and was a favourite fighter around the reservation, and had been a star wrestler in school. After graduating from Cass Lake High in 1992 he joined the army and became part of the elite Army Scouts, 25th Infantry Division, Schofield Barracks,

Hawaii. He loved it. But home was the Leech Lake Reservation and the network of family and friends and the land and landscape of northern Minnesota, where the boreal forest meets the oak savannah and where whites and Indians have been meeting and mixing since the early seventeenth century to fight, to trade, to bargain, to fuck and to marry.

Sam was, by any standard, a success. In 2002, Indians made up 1 per cent of Minnesota's population, and 7 per cent of the prison population. Indian men were 30 per cent more likely to go to jail than whites. The unemployment rate at Leech Lake Reservation was 46 per cent. Since 2008 it has risen to 60 per cent. The median household income is now less than $10,000 a year. Sam had avoided becoming one of those sour statistics that are rolled out to account for the perceived misery of reservation life. He had graduated. He had avoided jail. He had succeeded in getting a good, rewarding job. But he was homesick.

Then his sister Nessa died. Her death – she was hit by an RV after she drove across two yards and onto the highway – was the first death of our generation among our sprawling clan of siblings and cousins. 'Me and Nessa weren't on the best of terms,' Sam says. 'The weird point is that she'd stole my girlfriend from me, that's why I was so mad. I mean, who does that?' Vanessa did. She always had: she was one of just three female cousins in a group of about twenty or thirty males, and grew up scrappy and lippy. She was thin and pretty, and when she laughed she threw her chin up really high, almost like she was barking. She learned early on to tear up the scenery. She'd lived wild, like she was indestructible. But she wasn't.

When she died the family, almost visibly, deflated. Suddenly all that separated Sam from everyone else (graduation, a job, a life) disappeared. Like many Indians, he had no college safety net, or working parents, or a scrim of wealth or entitlement, or even the illusion that what he did, his work, or effort, counted for something, mattered in some way. He felt, as more and more Americans do, totally powerless. He didn't re-enlist and, instead, came back to Leech

Lake Reservation. He was angry; he drank and he fought. I remember seeing Sam around town those years. It seemed like every time I ran into him he had one less tooth, a new cast on his hand, a new scar. Back when we were kids he had a round, open, cheerful face, always laughing. He was the youngest of our set. Once in a while I'd pull him around by his hair. My brother and I saved him from drowning once, when he rode his Big Wheel into a pit filled with water from a broken water main. He was good-natured about the teasing, and good-natured about being saved. He was a brave kid – willing to do whatever we asked *because* we asked. When I close my eyes and hold him in my mind it is his boy's face that comes to me: smiling, dirt-smudged, eager.

But shortly after his return to the rez that boy's face, the face I'd known as well as my own growing up, disappeared and in its place appeared the hard face of a man who liked to fight, who liked hurting people. And he was a good street fighter. 'There were a few guys who'd work me over when I tangled with them, but not many. I won most of those fights. I don't know if that got me into the cage or not. But I got a taste for fighting.'

III. A taste for blood

Our tribe, the Ojibwe, are not known for being warlike. This is due to time and the nature of our victims: mostly we killed other Indians – Dakota, Sac and Fox, Cree. And our battles took place before the Plains Wars between the United States and tribes like the Cheyenne, Dakota, Lakota and Blackfeet. Everyone imagines that frontier violence was defined by Cowboys vs Indians. In reality, there were a lot of Indians vs Indians battles, long before the Plains Wars. The Ojibwe were fierce warriors, most unkind to our enemies. Until the late seventeenth century we didn't engage in much warfare beyond small skirmishes. Loose bands, based on marriage and clan, moved seasonally between beds of wild rice, fishing grounds and sugar bush. Hunger was the main enemy. As the demand for furs increased in the east and overseas, however, the Ojibwe around the Great Lakes acted as middlemen, securing furs from the west and selling them to the east in exchange for guns and ammunition and cloth. Our land base grew by a factor of twenty, infant mortality went down, standards of living went up and the small Ojibwe bands joined together into a vast, complicated, calculating tribe that controlled a major part of the fur trade.

The tribe was born of trade and came of age in blood, not on horseback on the plains, but on foot and by canoe in the deep woods and scattered watersheds of present-day Wisconsin and Minnesota. In an effort to expand our territory the Ojibwe began battling the Dakota. Life was war, and anyone who belonged to an enemy band was a legitimate target: men, women and children were killed, and scalped. Once, in order to show their disdain for Ojibwe warriors, a victorious party of Dakota refused to scalp the Ojibwe corpses. The Ojibwe, upon finding their dead untouched, flew into a rage. During one attack at Lake Mille Lacs in the seventeenth century the Ojibwe descended on a Dakota village and threw bags of gunpowder down the smoke holes of the enemy's lodges. The Dakota, burned and still burning, fled, only to be shot down. Hundreds died. As late as 2 April 1850, a party of Dakota from Red Wing, belonging to Little Crow's camp, attacked and killed some Ojibwe at a sugar camp near the St Croix River north-east of Stillwater, Minnesota. They killed and scalped fourteen Ojibwe and took a nine-year-old boy prisoner. The next day they paraded the bloody scalps and their young captive through the village of Stillwater to the horror of the white inhabitants. The Ojibwe chief, Bagonegiizhig (Hole-in-the-Day), was so incensed that in May 1850 he killed and scalped a Dakota man in front of his entire family in broad daylight on a Saint Paul street, and escaped with his entourage by canoe.

Bagonegiizhig was not the only Ojibwe war chief famous for his daring. Curly Head, Loon's Foot, Bad Boy, Flat Mouth, White Cloud – they were all fighters. But perhaps the most impressive Ojibwe warrior was Waabojiig, the White Fisher. As near as anyone can figure he was born in 1747, and showed courage and a warrior's sensibilities at a young age. During a battle with the Dakota, his father, Mangizid, made peace when he saw that among his enemies was his half-brother, the Dakota chief Wabasha. They ceased firing, and Mangizid invited his brother into his lodge. Waabojiig, who had been taught that the Dakota were the enemy, hid behind the door flap and when Wabasha stooped to enter, he hit him with all his might over the head with a war club. Wabasha rubbed his head and looked down at Waabojiig. 'My nephew!' he said. 'You're a brave one and I'm sure you'll go on to kill many of the enemy some day.' Waabojiig was eight years old at the time.

His uncle was right. By the time Waabojiig was in his early twenties he was already a war chief. 'In person,' wrote Ojibwe historian William Warren, 'Waabojiig was tall, being six feet six inches, erect in carriage and of slender make. He possessed a commanding countenance, united in ease and dignity of manners. He was a ready and fluent speaker . . .' One summer's campaign down the St Croix Valley against the Dakota he killed seventy-three of the enemy, most of them with his war club. The White Fisher is Sam's great-great-great-grand-uncle. Fighting, clearly, is in his blood.

But what to do when the fighting is over? What to do after open hostilities between the US government and tribes ended? What to do after the reservation period began and the martial spirit that had ensured our survival became an accessory to everyday life rather than its guarantor? Many twentieth-century Indians joined the US military. Indians had already served (sometimes with and sometimes against the US) in every major conflict since the Revolutionary War. In the twentieth century Indians signed up for and fought in every major overseas conflict, and served with distinction. Many Ojibwe, raised on the stories of their fathers and grandfathers, walked across the border to Canada and enlisted in the Canadian Expeditionary Force in order to see combat in World War I. They enlisted enthusiastically in the lead-up to World War II. To this day, a greater percentage of Indians have served in the military than any other group in America.

There are certainly socio-economic reasons for this: Indians are largely frozen out of the workforce. For as much as America might believe in assimilation (and that was certainly federal Indian policy for quite some time), assimilation begins from the bottom: you never really 'belong' to the country except as a labourer. The military was one of very few careers open to Indians in the first half of the twentieth century. There are also tribal, social and spiritual values that lead men (and women) into the military – certain ceremonial positions can only be held by veterans who have 'touched blood', which is a way to say that they have killed an enemy with their hands. Other cultural or social values – such as beauty, or tranquillity – are different on the rez. To be handsome, in the conventional sense, is not nearly as compelling as being tough. Having a tolerance for a particular kind of chaos is also a virtue. The Ojibwe motto might be: 'You can't win if you don't fight.'

I wonder, too: maybe we have lived lives of struggle and so have become *good* at violence. Violence is often thought of as the absence of culture, or its opposite: something that happens when societies fall apart. But perhaps violence is like everything else – something we learn, something we practise and something we can become good at. It is, for some of my tribe, their only marketable skill. But wars end. Other social values inflect reservation life now – the need for a steady income, and the incompatibility of constant aggression and chaos with wage labour. So what's an Indian man to do? What was Sam to do after his sister's death and the end of his four years in the army?

IV. Sam Cleveland's dark days

What Sam did was, by his own admission, two things – fight for no purpose, and commit crime. He was living in our ancestral village of Bena at the time. Leech Lake Reservation is a big reservation, about forty by forty miles. Within the reservation boundaries there are towns and villages tucked here and there among the swamps, rivers, lakes and pine trees. Some of the communities are almost exclusively Indian, like Inger and Ball Club, and some are almost all white. And some, like Bena, are decidedly mixed. Bena used to be a going concern – it was the end of the line during logging days so all sorts of timber outfits would get the train as far as Bena and then head north to their logging camps. After most of the virgin-white pine and pulp was cut down in northern Minnesota the town managed to stay alive through the growing tourist trade. As roads got better, boats sturdier and Americans wealthier, people travelled farther and farther north in search of good fishing. Situated on the southern shore of Lake Winnibigoshish, Bena became a fishing destination, sometimes swelling to a population in the high hundreds during the summer. But the lake got overfished, and Bena got smaller and smaller. Today it has one gas station, a bar and a post office. The hotels, hardware stores, restaurants, the school – all of it is gone. What has remained are a few big families descended from the mix of Ojibwe Indians and the Scots, English and Irish who came to cut trees and later to take people fishing on the beautiful waters of Lake Winnie. The Seelyes and Matthewses and Lyonses and Tibbettses and Dunhams and Michauds and Dormans and Drews. The population of Bena is around 140.

As much as Sam was drawn back to the reservation and to Bena out of loneliness and affection and despite the seemingly unbreakable bonds the village exerts on those of us whose families are from there, it can be a place that encourages destruction and dysfunction. Sam fought at bars. He fought at house parties. He fought in parking lots. He fought up and down the streets of Bena until he was too hurt and exhausted to continue.

He also drank a lot. His mother, my aunt Barb, who – like Sam – had done well (stable marriage, fairly good employment, comfortable homes), began to slide after Vanessa's death. Sober for years, she started drinking and using again. A host of health problems ensued. You can't use heroin, crack, scrips, pot, booze and cigarettes alternately and all together for very long before your body (and then your mind) quits on you. When I was a kid Barb was one of those aunties who always had a hug for you, who always laughed, who was always good for a piece of frybread at the powwow. She was one of the few who could make my mother laugh hard. But now the drugs used her. They ate away at her body. They ate away at her mind. Shortly before her death I walked past her at the Cass Lake powwow and didn't recognize her until she called my name and stood in front of me. There was nothing Sam could do about his sister or his mother except fight and that's what he did. Fighting and partying led to drugs and crime and a combination of the two. This life went on for years. It was a wonder *he* didn't die. But Sam had always had stamina. From 1996 till 2002 his life was a downward spiral, and it kept going down and down until he was sent to prison.

There was a rival group, one can't really call them a gang, who were dealing drugs around Bemidji. Skinheads. 'We were involved in a little drug ring, I guess you could say. These skinheads ripped off the guys I was with. And we went over there to that trailer park across from the mall in Bemidji, Pine Ridge trailer park, and I kicked down the door.' The subsequent violence led to eight months in prison. I wasn't sure what would happen to him after that. I didn't imagine it would be good.

But he did have people rooting for him. They began pulling him out of the rut he'd fallen into. 'Keevin Losh used to come visit me when I was in prison at Lino Lakes. He was a buddy of mine from high school. A fellow wrestler. He said to me, "Hey, I got you a job when you get out. I got you into the ironworkers' union." I didn't go back to Bena.' He was working hard, living away from the reservation and around that time, in 2002, he heard about MMA, mixed martial arts, on the radio.

v. Entering the cage

'I was sitting around one night listening to the radio,' says Sam, 'and this advertisement came on for "First Blood Ultimate Wrestling at the Lion's Den in Fridley". The ad said "local fighters wanted" and there was a number to call. This was in the beginning of the week. I went down there to talk to the guy – Brad Kohler, he became my promoter – on Thursday and I fought my first fight on Saturday. I didn't know anything. I just showed up with a nut cup and a mouth guard. I was about 165 pounds and my opponent was 195. I was scared. I didn't know what to expect. They walk you down this long hallway. You don't know what's at the other end of it. I didn't know what to expect at all. The Lion's Den was just this little underground place and they threw a cage up in the middle of it and packed a few hundred people in there and then put two guys in the cage and let 'em go. Didn't even matter if they were matched up good or even the same size or anything. A lot of mismatches that day. It was pretty wild. This was February 2002.'

From the start, MMA was about two things: spectacle and money. It began as a promotional stunt to advertise Brazilian ju-jitsu. Advertiament more than true athleticism. Although these tough-man challenges had been staged all over the world, MMA came to the US in 1993 as the Ultimate Fighting Championship held in Denver, Colorado, at the McNichols Sports Arena. There was one round with no time limits, arranged tournament style – single elimination rounds, leading up to a final. The logic of the spectacle was in part that of mismatching: could a boxer beat a wrestler, a wrestler a kickboxer? What about kung fu and tae kwon do? What is ju-jitsu and what is Brazilian ju-jitsu? How would a 170-pound street fighter fare against a 400-pound sumo wrestler? It advertised itself as having one rule: *There are no rules!* This was almost true. Bare-fisted, the fighters were allowed to punch, kick, elbow, knee, pull hair, fishhook (put a finger in the corner of your opponent's mouth and pull), groin strike, headbutt and kick a guy on the ground. It was bloody and it was destructive and it was riveting.

Senator John McCain didn't think so, and after UFC 1 he lobbied lawmakers to ban it. Thirty-six states did. A lot of the fighters went overseas and the UFC almost folded. But it came back when it was purchased by a pair of casino owners and an MMA manager named

Dana White for the sum of $2 million. Really the only thing they were buying was the name – it had no assets and no contracts, nothing at all except for those three letters and a large underground following. They instituted a few rules – no groin hits, headbutting, biting, hair pulling and no knees or kicks to the head when your opponent is on the ground. They instituted rounds, usually five-minute rounds, and all matches were 'singles matches'. Fighters would only fight once a day and they'd know months in advance who the other guy was and could train specifically for a fight against a person who had known strengths and weaknesses. No longer would fighters show up in plain shorts or in a gi without even so much as a mouth guard. No longer would teeth fly out of people's mouths to land under the announcers' table. No longer would people's shorts and T-shirts be the kind you could buy at Shopko or Play It Again Sports.

The fighters (and the fights) began to look more professional. Sponsors got into the game. By early 2002 the UFC was on its way to becoming the dominant circuit in the fastest-growing sport in the world. Other leagues weren't so legit. Pride, K-1, Strikeforce, International Fight League, EliteXC, Bellator Fighting Championships, and smaller leagues such as World Extreme Cagefighting (WEC), Art of War, Adrenaline MMA, Ohio Xtreme Fighting, Fight, EFC, Combate Extremo, King of the Cage, Icon, Cyper, US-MMA and Gladiator Challenge. These smaller outfits were as keen to bring in spectators, to sell tickets, and for the promoters and arrangers to develop talent, as the UFC had been – even to the detriment of the fighters themselves.

One way promoters and agents have of developing talent is to sacrifice new blood to the old, giving their established guy a better record and more experience with little risk. The new fighters sometimes don't fall under the bus as much as they are placed there. This, at first, is what happened to Sam. He lost the first fight that Saturday in February 2002. He lost his second fight, too. But he won the third, against an experienced opponent. He knew then that he could be an MMA fighter.

Sam quit his job and moved down to Moline, Illinois, where his father Jerry was living. Pat Miletech, a former UFC champion, had opened an MMA gym close by in Bettendorf, on the Iowa side of the Mississippi. Sam trained there for two months and learned the basics alongside fighters such as Matt Hughes, Jens Pulver and Tim Sylvia. He didn't feel like an outsider. He knew he could hang with the other guys, not a few of whom were or would be world champions. Everything was looking up until Sam's mother, Barb, died after a suicide attempt in the summer of 2005.

VI. Sammy's fight

On a summer night in 2005 Barb locked herself in her house, called her brothers and said she was going to kill herself. The police arrived and together with Barb's brothers, my uncles, they broke down the door when they heard a shot fired. Barb had grazed her ribs with a single shot from a .30-.30 deer rifle. The wound wasn't life-threatening. Nor, unbelievably, did she have drugs in her system. It looked as though she would survive but the ambulance took her to the Indian Health Service clinic as per policy – all ambulance calls on the reservation, no matter how dire, are sent to the clinic first, whether a doctor is there or not, rather than to the large regional hospital fourteen miles down the road in Bemidji. This is policy only because it saves the government money. When Barb was admitted to the clinic the physician's assistant (there was no MD present) misread her vitals and the charts and intubated her. This would have been fine, except he accidentally shoved the breathing tube into her stomach, which compressed her lungs, and when her lungs began to collapse he pumped more air into her stomach. She died on the table while my mother and brother waited for news in the waiting room.

We all wondered what would happen to Sam. But he stayed in control and kept his job, and didn't drift back into the violence that had marked his life for most of his twenties. 'I had a life and a family and I was fighting. I left all my anger in the cage.' Maybe he does leave it all there. But if he does, he *brings* something to the cage as well. 'It feels good to win,' he says. 'It feels good to win at something you've worked hard at, to win at something you want real bad.' More than anything, that's what Sam and a lot of the other Indian fighters bring to fighting in the cage: the desire to be good at something, and to have a chance to win on the basis of talent and hard work. It may sound like a small thing. To me it sounds like the very idea – meritocracy – that America is built on. But it is a huge thing for an Indian man to *want*, a huge and noble thing to dare to *hope* that hard work and talent will actually win the day.

In the end, Sam didn't get to fight on 17 March 2012. His opponent failed to make weight at 160 and wanted to enter the ring at 175 pounds. Sam said no. He'd been mismatched early in his career when he didn't know better. He wasn't going to sacrifice himself now – not even for us, his family, his friends, his reservation. Not in that way at least. He had too much respect for himself to put himself at risk. And I was proud of him. I was proud of the man he'd become; the one who had thought hard enough and worked hard enough and cared about himself enough to make a tough decision. I had wanted to see him fight. But I was proud of him.

Earlier, in December, I *had* gotten to see him fight – a fight organized by the King of the Cage and held at Northern Lights Casino. I had the same dizzy feeling at that fight as I did later in March – the same mix of fighters, some of whom were amazing, and some you couldn't help worry about as you would worry about a younger brother or defenceless child. The Cage Girls were there. The coaches and corner men. Some were professional, others looked like they were doing deals when they were talking to their fighters. Sam had won against a much larger opponent in the first two minutes of the first round in his trademark style – he took him down, mounted him and punched his opponent in the face until he gave up. He had seemed unstoppable. God how he could hit. How could a man like him lose? How could he ever lose?

Watching him then I simply couldn't imagine him doing anything other than winning. I didn't have the words for it: what it felt like to watch my cousin, whom I love and whose worries are our worries and whose pain is our pain, manage to be so good at something, to triumph so completely. More than a painful life, more than a member of a culture that has perfected living through violence, making it a virtue because it is a necessity, more than a meanness or a willingness to sacrifice oneself, what I felt, what I *saw*, were Indian men and boys doing precisely what we've always been taught *not* to do. I was seeing them plainly, desperately, expertly, want to be applauded for their subversive talents and hard work. This was as true for those who lost as much as for those who won. And – beaming, cheering, clapping, wholly caught up in the victory of desire itself – I have never been more proud. That old feeling familiar to so many Indians – that we can't change anything, can't change Columbus or Custer, smallpox or massacres, the Gatling gun or the legislative act, the loss of our loved ones or the birth of new troubles, the feeling that we can't change a thing about the shape and texture of our lives fell away completely. Watching the fighters it occurred to me: we might actually win.

I think the same could be said for Sam: he might not have been able to change his sister's fate or his mother's or even, for a while, his own. But when he stepped into the cage he was doing battle with a disease. The disease was the feeling of powerlessness that takes hold of even the most powerful Indian men. For three rounds of five minutes you get to prove that you can determine the outcome of a finite struggle. Win or lose. Hit or be hit. He could control that. Sam dominated his opponent under the bright, artificial lights of the Northern Lights Casino as Waabojiig and all the other chiefs and warriors dominated their enemies before him. ∎

© DANIEL JOSEPH MARTINEZ
I Can't Imagine Ever Wanting To Be White, 1993
Courtesy of the artist and Roberts & Tilton, Culver City, California

A CONFESSION

Jess Row

I'm going to say something here that should come as no surprise, at least not to those of my generation, born after the civil rights movement had shrunk to pages 263–7 of *American Panoramas*, and raised, for the most part, in the eighties, watching Bill Cosby sell Pudding Pops on TV: my education in blackness, in the experience of black people in America, began one hot summer afternoon in 1989, in sticky-floored Theater C at the Chestnut Hill Mall 13, with Spike Lee's *Do the Right Thing*.

Of course I had heard rap before. I knew, in a kind of academic way, what a crack addict was, and I knew a great deal about Martin Luther King: my parents' first date was at the March on Washington in 1963. But in the world I lived in before I moved to Baltimore – Newton, Massachusetts, *not* Boston, unless you count the occasional trip to the Aquarium or Faneuil Hall – the only black people I saw regularly were babysitters and maids. My parents were ardent Democrats, classic north-eastern liberals, who nonetheless, characteristically, chose to live in a neighbourhood populated with people exactly like themselves – plus a margin of Chinese, Indian, Thai and garden-variety reform Ashkenazim – for the schools, the parks, the playgrounds, the excellent restaurants.

Of course it wasn't Alabama, it wasn't 1955; there were always a few black kids, a photogenic sprinkling. Tiffany and Wesley Roberts, whose father was Duane Roberts, the Celtics point guard, were one year ahead of me at Passing Brook Elementary. Tiffany was grasshopper-legged, a natural sprinter, an indefatigable four-square champion; Wesley spent recesses under the pines at the far end of the soccer field, trading stickers, buttons, Garbage Pail Kids, baseball cards, Dungeons & Dragons imaginary weapons – whatever currency of the moment.

That was where I came to know him, briefly, in third grade, before Duane was traded to the SuperSonics. He sat hunched over, legs folded, stretching out the hem of his long T-shirt like a table, displaying some treasure – a folder of Reggie Jackson cards from every season, a Don Mattingly rookie card, a mint Topps pack of the 1979 Pirates – and daring the rest of us to make an offer. It wasn't fun, exactly, being so utterly outmatched, but Wesley knew how to work the margins, trading cards he didn't need for the best we had to offer. He stared into space, over our shoulders, reciting statistics in a listless, deadpan voice, showing why his cards were always worth more, had more long-term potential; he used words like *investment* and *dividends*. Today we might give him a diagnosis – Asperger's, mild autism, social anxiety disorder – but no one at the time, as far as I can recall, saw anything wrong. Never did anyone in that circle refer to him as *black*. Creatures of instinct, we didn't care about the colour of his skin, or the content of his character; we cared about his stuff. Only later did it occur to me that that was why he sought us out, and perhaps why he became – I googled him once, in idle curiosity, a few years ago – a venture capitalist seeding start-ups and then selling them to Microsoft. He's grown into his looks now; he and his father have a foundation together that runs after-school sports programmes in Seattle.

This was the life I was raised to have, racially speaking, the life my parents had, post-1973, when they left Back Bay for the suburbs, the life of a Good White Person. I was meant to have a few, select, black friends – peers, confidants, individuals – a number of acquaintances, business associates, secretaries, hygienists, a few charities to which I would give generously, as much as possible, and a broad, sympathetic, detached view of the continuing struggles of African Americans to achieve the long-delayed goals of full civic participation, low birth rates, ascension to the middle class, hiring equity, educational parity and so, so, so, on, on, on. I was supposed to live with the frisson of guilt that comes from owning an expensive, elaborate security system, and to mention, at parties, that rates of incarceration for black males are six times the national average. I was supposed to organize for Obama, and own at least ten separate items of Obama paraphernalia, and proudly display my *Yes We Did* postcard on my refrigerator for all of 2009 and 2010, and feel that slow-fading flush of warmth and exultation, as if someone had reached out and grasped my hand, and held it, a squeeze as a substitute for an embrace. This was the life, until a few weeks ago, that I thought I was having. I should have known better.

*1*989 – *a number, another summer – sound of the funky drummer!*
What did I hear, that first time, when Donald Harrison's rendition of 'Lift Every Voice' ended, and 'Fight the Power' roared to life, in a cacophony of scratches, samples and found noise before that first deep bass hit, that nearly lifted me out of my chair? Something like the screeching of brakes, something like a jet plane taking off: that's what the Bomb Squad sounded like to a fourteen-year-old in 1989, who was used to the tinny, Casio-looped beats on eighties rap. Even before the story began, the credits were a body blow – the sheer brightness of the colours, the insistent, defiant, angry sidewalk dancing of Rosie Perez, in a red minidress and tights, in shiny boxer's trunks, bobbing and weaving. Everything that came after was a little after the fact of that first song. *Our freedom of speech is freedom or death. Elvis was a hero to most. But he never meant shit to me.*

I was listening. I was paying attention.

It wasn't long after that that the few black kids at Newton South

Middle started wearing T-shirts that said *It's a black thing – you wouldn't understand*. By this time I had graduated from the haze of childhood and had begun hanging out, whenever I could, in Harvard Square, and particularly in Newbury Comics, the epicentre of cool. My father was just then negotiating the terms of his new job at Black & Decker in Baltimore – he was, is, an electrical engineer, who invents power-saving devices for small appliances – and I knew my world was shifting, that Newton was already history, *over*, and I started turning my attention to magazines: *Spin, Rolling Stone, Alternative Press, Maximumrocknroll, Vibe*, the *Source*. And it was in *Spin* that I read an interview with Chuck D that contained the sentence *White liberals aren't our salvation, they're the problem*.

It had never occurred to me that I was someone else's problem.

With *Do the Right Thing* came Public Enemy. After Public Enemy came N.W.A., Niggaz Wit Attitudes. And at the same moment, the Native Tongues, De La Soul, A Tribe Called Quest, X Clan, Del the Funky Homosapien, the Pharcyde, Black Sheep, Arrested Development, Ice-T, Ice Cube, Onyx. In the early nineties, hip hop was everywhere but invisible – still controversial, still not quite accepted even as music, still hardly on the radio, and therefore an indispensable part of a teenager's education. By the time I was sixteen I was buying bootleg tapes of every new album, five dollars a pop, and I could repeat whole songs, whole sides of albums. It was the omega to punk's alpha, the nastiness to our earnestness. *Ends justifies the means, that's the system, so I don't celebrate no bullshit Thanksgiving*. I listened to it hypnotically, miming the gestures in traffic on the way to school, spraying my imaginary MAC-10 through the windshield. *It's the number-one crew in the area, make a move for your gat and I'll bury ya*.

This shit is pathetic, my friend Ayala Kauffmann said, once, a year later, when I was giving her a ride to school. She was biracial, though it was easy to miss; with a mop of brown curls, a nose ring and an Indian-print blouse she could have been any other Rebekah, Aviva or

Dasi. Hinjews, Mexijews, Sephardi ex-kibbutzniks – at Willow we had them all. Her father had disappeared when she was a baby, leaving nothing to her, not even his name, and her mother had remarried Ira Kauffmann, a balding, kindly Reform rabbi with fishy eyes.

I mean, she said, I get it. I get De La Soul. Everybody loves De La Soul. But this is just like looking at *Hustler*. It's *gross*. And it's grosser still because it's *you*. Nobody meant this for you. Or if they did, it's just a classic retread minstrel show. *Look at the bad black man!* You're getting played. I can't believe you would pay money for this shit.

I didn't. Well, not much, anyway.

And you think that makes it okay?

Just because you're not listening to it doesn't mean it's not out there, I said. Wouldn't you rather know?

What, this is supposed to be my direct line from the ghetto?

Chuck D says hip hop is the black world's CNN.

You're not the black world. You're not *black*, don't you get it? And listening to this shit doesn't change that. It just makes you a parasite. It would be one thing if you actually *knew* any black people. And I don't count.

That's really fair. You get to be the authority, but yet you don't count.

You don't get to decide what's fair, she said. Don't you understand? She ejected the tape before I could stop her and flipped it into the back seat, among the Subway wrappers and 7-Eleven coffee cups, the broken microphone stand and the guitar-string envelopes. You get to shut up, she said. That's your special job. You get to not have rights for a change. Shut up and go away and leave black people *alone*, for once.

I didn't listen. Or maybe, in some sense, I did.
At Willow, in place of community service, we had what we called *volunteer jobs*, assigned by the principal's office, six hours a week minimum. And the black people I knew in any true sense – any real recognition, any actual conversation – were all from my VJ shifts downtown: soup kitchen, sophomore year; food pantry, junior year; community health clinic, senior year. Mostly my supervisors were

solemn, tight-mouthed men, ex-cons, Vietnam vets, halfway-house residents, who hardly bothered to learn my name; but there were always others, who asked why I wore my hair that way, who wanted to know how many hours of community service I'd been sentenced to, and what I'd done to deserve it; who offered me menthol cigarettes, which I graciously, nauseously accepted; who told me something about doing a month in the hole at Lorton, or being shot out of a helicopter in Khe Sanh.

And then there was James, a category of his own. James supervised a whole crew of prep-school do-gooders – PSDGs, that was his term – at the Belinda Matthews Memorial Food Pantry on Saturday mornings, teaching us how to process a hundred pounds of cast-off lettuce, how to stack boxes of government cheese, how to load a shopping bag so it wouldn't split. He stood a head taller than most of us, six-five, in an army jacket, with a shining bald dome, a crocheted skullcap and a silvery soul patch, like an ageing hero from a Melvin Van Peebles movie. He told us he'd been in the same City College class with Kurt Schmoke, then the mayor; after that, he'd turned down a scholarship to Howard, travelled the country playing bass in an R&B band, and spent some time with the Peoples Temple in California, years before Jonestown. But I knew, even then, he said, more than once, I knew that Jim Jones was a crazy motherfucker. It was well *known* that he would screw anything that moved, anybody that came within ten feet. Man or woman. That was how he did it, you know. Everybody felt dirty. Everybody was compromised. Closer you get, the more compromised. So I packed my bags and got out of that scene.

And then what? Alan once asked him. We were on the same shift, in the fall of our junior year; we'd go straight from pitching rotten tomatoes to band practice. What'd you do then, after Jim Jones? How'd you get back to Baltimore?

James palmed a cantaloupe from a wax-board crate, sniffed it, like a chef looking for the peak of ripeness. Son, he said, looking straight at Alan, I did cocaine. Nothing but cocaine for fifteen years. You hear?

Bought, sold, sniffed, ate, shot up, smoked, stuck it on my gums, stuck it up my ass once. Took it into prison with me, took it right up to the moment I left. Fifteen years in the white mountains. Six of them in jail. Then I found God, and here we are.

I guess we should take that as a warning, Alan said.

No, James said, and he coughed politely to keep from laughing. I'm not here as a warning. Not to you.

He was a Muslim, though he rarely discussed it; not Nation of Islam, but NBIM, which, he told me once, stood for New Baltimore Integrated Mosque, a special congregation where Arabs and Pakistanis and black people all worshipped together. Occasionally, if I arrived early enough, I found him doing morning prayers outside in the empty lot next to the food pantry's row house. *Inshallah*, he always said, when we talked about how many bags we'd distribute that day, and Alan and I started doing it too, as a joke first, and then without thinking. *Inshallah*, we could sell fifteen T-shirts. *Inshallah*, you get into Wesleyan.

It happened to be in the same moment that I came to know James that I read *The Autobiography of Malcolm X* for the first time, and came upon the rapper Paris, who referred casually to *blue-eyed devils* and *sons of Yakub* as if talking about his uncle Bill from Indiana. At the Black Cat bookstore on Read Street, I found copies of *The Final Call* and the *New Afrikan Party Newsletter*, and sat reading, for an entire Sunday afternoon, one column of tiny print after another, mesmerized by explanations of how the downfall of White Amerikkka could be predicted by the phases of the sun, how school health clinics and Planned Parenthood were agents of genocide, how black people could use shea butter to boost their natural immunity to Aids.

There was something refreshing about being called a devil. This was in 1991, at the very peak of the crack wars, when Baltimore was Murder Capital for the first time; I had just gotten my licence, and I drove myself, alone, or sometimes with Alan, down to the food pantry twice or three times a week, and the fact of being independent changed everything I saw, as if I had to own the city for the first time, having to find my own parking spaces in it. It wasn't a matter of fear, though I carried Mace with me everywhere, wore my wallet and keys on a biker chain and checked the back seat and trunk of the car religiously, as carjackers were known to put a gun to your head from behind as you drove. What astonished me was how easily I could slip past the box hedges and pin oaks of Roland Park, the Victorians and Colonials and Tudors prim and quiet, and into the derelict corridors, the bombed-out storefronts, the vacants, the dealers in puffy jackets standing sentry on every corner, the Korean liquor stores with armoured grates and triple-thick glass in front of the register. This was a drive of ten minutes. It is still, come to think of it, a drive of ten minutes. This geography, I thought, was a crime. Someone had given me a postcard of Proudhon that I taped to my locker: *Property is theft.* How could it be anything else? How could I be anything other than a criminal, by the fact of my pimply existence?

I even started doing it with Alan. If gay people could be queers, what was the harm? What up, devil? I said to him once, within James's earshot, and James turned around.

Did you just say what I think you said?

You're right, Alan said. It's not funny.

You don't hear me calling anyone around here a nigger, do you?

You could if you wanted to.

Thanks, James said. Thanks for giving your permission.

That's not what I meant –

Lookit here, he snapped. We got a job to do. I watched, so clearly, as all his affection for us folded up in his face like a fan. No names, no name-calling.

Well, we are, aren't we?

Aren't we what?

Aren't we the devil? I mean, aren't we the *problem*?

He shrugged.

Choose, he said. Be the devil if you want. What you are right *now* is a pain in my ass who can't sort tomatoes worth a damn. This look ripe to you? Get back to your job, okay? Just do your *job*.

In October of the following year, our senior year, James was shot twice in the head in his apartment above the food pantry, and the building was torched; when I drove down, that same afternoon, it was still smoking, wound around with police tape, and the roof had caved in. I recognized one of our weekly clients, Dawson, wheeling a shopping cart filled with neatly sorted bags of beer bottles and aluminum cans. Hell, he said, you didn't know? Motherfucker was selling drugs out of there the whole time. Wednesday through Friday, when the pantry was closed. Went in there one time myself, see if I could get me some extra cans of beans. Didn't want none of *those* kinds of beans, feel me? Yeah, he had a good thing going there for a while.

I don't believe it, I said.

Then forget it, he said. Forget I said anything. Don't matter now, do it? Still dead. Still fucked it up for the rest of us. Got to go down to Jonah House now, stand in line.

I'll give you a ride, I said. It felt, obscurely, like being at the end of a TV movie; I was supposed to have learned something. I was supposed to be changed. Black people's lives, I should have said, facing the camera, are no more expressive of statistics than anyone else's. Who am I, who are *you*, to go looking in this horror for a pattern?

Naw, Dawson said. Can't leave the cart.

Put it in the trunk.

Everything's going to turn out all right, he said, pushing away from me. Trust in the Lord. You hear me?

When I went to college I snapped out of my love of hip hop, as if out of a dream. Someone looked at my tape collection and laughed. Who are you supposed to be, homeboy? I dumped them all in a box and began buying CDs instead – Pavement, the Spinanes, Stereolab, Liz Phair. I grew a goatee, developed a taste for expensive coffee, read Baudrillard and John Ashbery, read Ginsberg and Williams and Pound, read Rexroth and Kerouac and D.T. Suzuki, and began getting up at seven thirty for daily Chinese classes.

Was I fleeing from something? Was I certain why I loved this new language, with its four tones and 80,000 characters, its unshakeable alienness, its irreconcilability with any language, any world, I knew? Is that even a question? Did any of us know why, given all our advantages, our entitlements, our good study habits and chemically inflated self-esteem, we were still so prone to spastic fits of despair, why we sought out more and more exotic ways of getting high, why we wore Sanskrit rings and tribal tattoos, salon-styled dreadlocks and Japanese see-through raincoats? How could it be running away, when it was nothing more than running in place? How could it be guilt, when the air was so thick with good intentions, with accusations and counter-accusations?

All I know is this: when I came home, I never went downtown. I tore my *Illmatic* poster off my bedroom wall and used the back for calligraphy practice. In a fit of orderly pique, I carted off the contents of my high-school bookcase – *Invisible Man, Native Son, The Fire Next Time, The Autobiography of Malcolm X, Beware Soul Brother, Black Like Me, Black Ice, I Know Why the Caged Bird Sings* – to the Salvation Army. I waited, listening, for the thunderclap, the world splitting open under my feet, and heard only the tinkling of the Good Humor truck down the block, the moan of Mr Takematsu's ageing lawnmower over the backyard fence. I thought of my parents' earnest faces, of my father, clean-shaven, playing the guitar for my kindergarten class – *If I had a hammer, I'd hammer out danger ... I'd hammer out love between my brothers and my sisters all over this land* – and their sententious, balsamic-sprinkling, Chablis-swilling, late middle age, their faces puckered with concern over the prospect that I would go off to China and become a mercenary investment banker. How vicious and unfair to blame them for my lack of imagination, with the short and pathetic half-life of my good intentions! When all I wanted, all any of us wanted, was to go back to that childlike state, hand-holding, faces raised to the words of the beatific saint, promising us that this story, like all good stories, had an ending, that everything was going to be okay.

What is there in Mookie's face, when he staggers away from the scene of Radio Raheem's death, picks up the garbage can and carries it, like a javelin thrower, to its launching point, to the window of Sal's Famous? Why, that is, doesn't he have any expression at all? As if he's watching his life flash by on TV. As if he's watching an old, old movie. His whole body sags with the effort of acting out the script. And I, even then, even at fourteen, knew that I was supposed to hate him, and couldn't. And wanted to *be* him, and couldn't. *Here we go again,* his face says. *I don't want you to witness this.* He is alone. He doesn't want to be the Representative Black Man. But he can't be anything else. The credits roll; I wipe my popcorn-greasy hands on my shorts. I walk out of the theatre in a daze. I've glimpsed something. But a glimpse, as it turns out, is not enough.

I lived in white dreamtime. I have been living in white dreamtime. And the problem with dreaming, the epistemological problem, is: when you think you've woken up, have you really? Is this waking, or a deeper, more profound state of sleep, the state of the most vivid and palpable dreams?

There's something else I forgot. Or, rather, something else I can't remember. I can't remember what caused me to fight the boy; I was seven, we were at some school summer camp, not in Newton but nearby; he appeared out of nowhere, and like that we were grappling in the dust, the only fight I'd had in my life up to that time. He elbowed me in the shoulder, pushed me over and walked off; I was blinded, howling. That nigger, I said, when my counsellor picked me up, and he put me down immediately and pinned me against the wall by my shoulders. Don't *ever* say that again, he said. He had greasy shoulder-length black hair, a knobby nose, a Ziggy Stardust T-shirt fraying at the collar. You understand? Say it again and I'll beat the shit out of you myself. I'll fucking *kill* you. You understand?

How is anyone supposed to understand?

Thus ends my confession. ■

CASTA

Nicola Lo Calzo

U p until the start of the Civil War, three main castes organized
society in the states of Louisiana and Mississippi: white Creoles
of French and Spanish descent; Creoles of colour (free men and
women of mixed African and European descent); and enslaved
people of African descent.

After the Civil War, the caste system was gradually replaced by
segregation, which preserved hierarchy based on skin colour by
imposing only two racial categories: whites and blacks. But this new
system did not correspond to the fragmented and complex social
reality.

Today, physical proximity does not translate into interaction
between communities. More often than not, communities remain
separated while laying claim to different aspects of a heritage or
tradition. During interviews, the common denominator is constant
reference to the Civil War. The war divides the world. There is on one
hand a celebration of the good old antebellum days when Louisiana's
upper class was among the richest in the country – as evidenced in the
Natchez Garden Club and leisure tourism on former plantations. On
the other hand there is the remembrance of slavery and segregation,
as can be seen in the Zulu Social Aid & Pleasure Club, St Peter Claver
Church and Black Indian tribes.

I decided to undertake this research documentary project to
better understand the origin of this racialized geography. I wanted
to investigate how historical racial categories shape memory, heritage
and political and interpersonal relations. ■

Translated by Prince Ofori-Atta

1. Bettye Jenkins, Hawthorne House, Natchez, Mississippi

2. Brandon and Wallace waiting for the Zulu parade organized by
the Zulu Social Aid & Pleasure Club, Hilton Hotel, New Orleans

3. Members of the Bunch Club, one of the city's oldest African American fraternal organizations, with special guests, before the annual Bunch Club Carnival Dance, Hyatt Regency Hotel, New Orleans

4. Artistic Director Akeem Martin presenting *Not Unto Us*, a play about Black Reconstruction, written by Clifford Graves in 1940, George & Leah McKenna Museum of African American Art, New Orleans

5. David Ducros, rap singer, during the filming of '1 Mic', Tremé, New Orleans

6. Second line parade in Tremé, New Orleans

7. The Sisters of the Holy Family congregation, founded in 1842 in New Orleans

8. Katarina Boudreaux, Cajun singer, descendant of French settler Michel Boudreaux, Garden District, New Orleans

9. Maurepas Swamp, Louisiana

10. Diane H. Destrehan, a tour guide integrating the history of slavery into plantation tours, at the end of a tour at her ancestors' house, Destrehan Plantation, Louisiana

11. Noah, Confederate Infantry, Civil War re-enactment at Fort Randolph, Pineville, Louisiana

12. Sir Boxley dressed as a Civil War soldier at the Forks of the Road, historical site of the enslavement market, Natchez, Mississippi

13. Slave cabin, Felicity Plantation, Vacherie, Louisiana

14. Ricardo, member of the Buffalo Soldiers, Claiborne Avenue, Tremé, New Orleans

15. Supporters taking photographs of the Hard Head Hunters tribe during a Mardi Gras parade, Bywater District, New Orleans

16. Charice Harrison-Nelson, Queen of the Guardians of the Flame tribe, celebrating the memory of African slaves, Tomb of the Unknown Slave, St Augustine Catholic Church, Tremé, New Orleans

17. David Montana, Big Chief of the Washitaw Nation, Tremé, New Orleans

18. Alphonse Robair, member of the Hard Head Hunters tribe, Bywater District, New Orleans

19. Guests at the Mardi Gras Rex Ball, Sheraton Hotel, New Orleans

20. Oaks, Natchez, Mississippi

GO WILD

Subscribe to *Granta* to save up to 38% on the cover price and get free access to the magazine's entire digital archive.

Complete the form overleaf,
visit granta.com or call +44 (0)208 955 7011

UK

£36 | £32 by Direct Debit

EUROPE

£42

REST OF THE WORLD*

£46

*US, Canada and Latin America not included

'An indispensable part
of the intellectual landscape'
—*Observer*

GRANTA.COM

© CRISTINA DE MIDDEL

GRANTA

THE MAGAZINE OF NEW WRITING

SUBSCRIPTION FORM FOR UK, EUROPE AND REST OF THE WORLD

Yes, I would like to take out a subscription to *Granta*.

GUARANTEE: If I am ever dissatisfied with my *Granta* subscription, I will simply notify you, and you will send me a complete refund or credit my credit card, as applicable, for all un-mailed issues.

YOUR DETAILS

MR / MISS / MRS / DR ....

NAME ....

ADDRESS ....

....

POSTCODE ....

EMAIL ....

☐ Please tick this box if you do not wish to receive special offers from *Granta*
☐ Please tick this box if you do not wish to receive offers from organizations selected by *Granta*

YOUR PAYMENT DETAILS

1) ☐ Pay £32 (saving £20) by Direct Debit
   To pay by Direct Debit please complete the mandate and return to the address shown below.

2) Pay by cheque or credit/debit card. Please complete below:

   1 year subscription: ☐ UK: £36   ☐ Europe: £42   ☐ Rest of World: £46

   3 year subscription: ☐ UK: £99   ☐ Europe: £108   ☐ Rest of World: £126

   I wish to pay by ☐ CHEQUE ☐ CREDIT/DEBIT CARD
   Cheque enclosed for £ _____ made payable to *Granta*.

   Please charge £ _____ to my: ☐ Visa ☐ MasterCard ☐ Amex ☐ Switch/Maestro

   Card No. ☐☐☐☐☐☐☐☐☐☐☐☐☐☐☐☐☐☐

   Valid from *(if applicable)* ☐☐ / ☐☐   Expiry Date ☐☐ / ☐☐   Issue No. ☐☐

   Security No. ☐☐☐

SIGNATURE .... DATE ....

Instructions to your Bank or Building Society to pay by Direct Debit

BANK NAME ....

BANK ADDRESS ....

POSTCODE ....

ACCOUNT IN THE NAMES(S) OF: ....

SIGNED ....

DATE ....

DIRECT Debit

Instructions to your Bank or Building Society: Please pay Granta Publications direct debits from the account detailed on this instruction subject to the safeguards assured by the direct debit guarantee. I understand that this instruction may remain with Granta and, if so, details will be passed electronically to my bank/building society. Banks and building societies may not accept direct debit instructions from some types of account.

Bank/building society account number

☐☐☐☐☐☐☐☐

Sort Code

☐☐☐☐☐☐

Originator's Identification

9 1 3 1 3 3

Please mail this order form with payment instructions to:

Granta Publications
12 Addison Avenue
London, W11 4QR
Or call +44(0)208 955 7011
Or visit GRANTA.COM for details

A Meeting of Minds with Henry David Thoreau

1. Into the Wood

When I arrived in that new country for the first time
I came by boat,
by canoe in fact and completely alone,
so the pines and conifers stepping down to the river,
some with their roots as pink as pigs' tails
in the dark current swirling around them regardless,
were my only company.

It was for this reason perhaps
I found myself striking my double-ended paddle
hard against the side of my canoe:
to frighten them away
if such a thing were possible.

Also to start echoes,
and to have those echoes multiply
and fill the woods with circles of dilating sound,
awakening the trees.

Stirring up, I could call it,
as might be done to animals and people,
and to make all melodies a replica
of things they know already,
and the places where they find them.

2. Finds

Their spears are very serviceable –
the pointed part a hemlock knot,
and the side-spring pieces of hickory –
for use on salmon, pickerel, trout, chub, etc.,
unless
by the light of birch-fires after sunset
it is converted into a pole or club.

These were my original discoveries.

After that:
a sled, or *jebongon*, carved from thin wood
turned up at the front and drawn by a strong bark rope.

A cradle.

A canoe much more convenient than my own.

A vessel for water, or for boiling meat with hot stones.

And arrow-heads,
that lie through the woods like expectation,
over the whole face of America.

Stone fruit I thought,
but soon afterwards frost flowers
that still appear to my eye
and are cold to my touch
when the frost itself wears off,
and the ground is bare.

3. Travellers

I planted out the first potatoes today,
when I was not reading F.A. Michaux,
the younger Michaux that is,
describing himself on the shore of the Monogahala
as five or six bateaux,
filled with horses, cattle, pigs, poultry,
dismounted carts,
ploughs,
harnesses and beds
presented in turn their ends,
their sides,
their angles
to the current that swept them on to their destination.

Looking up from the page and around my cabin,
in which I can now safely say that I have come to rest,
I was put in mind of a friend
who recently broke into the grasslands
and was impeded for a day
by a herd of bison fifty miles long
and three miles wide.

When he followed them to a ford
the gravel underfoot
was covered with moulted hair to a depth of six inches.

4. Moonlight

I remind myself when I reach the pond at sunset
how far water reveals itself by night,

as the moon shimmering across the surface,
tightens into a pyramid of light
that points to me,
that points me out indeed
and, in the same gesture,
also burns the crests of small waves
with flames I thought at first were fireflies.

We do not habitually live our lives in full;
we do not fill ourselves sufficiently with blood.

Even so, as they creep close and closer still to me
I see those flames increase,
so many broken fragments of the moon
they seem more intense than the moon itself,
until their brightness makes me turn away,
and wish for company
to share my task of looking,
and the light complete.

5. The Axe

I threw my axe behind me towards the lake
and being filled with the involuntary life of things
it skimmed some twenty yards across the ice
and then dropped in
through a hole that I had recently made there myself.

I crawled back out,
and saw it twenty-five feet down,
the handle upright,
swaying in the bright clear water

as if the water or the axe itself
had discovered a pulse.

Which decided me.

I made a device of birch and rope,
hooked the axe after several attempts,
raised it,
seized it,
and so brought it home.

I found in my absence that I had missed two visitors:
one left me nothing I could know them by;
the other
must have been a woman,
judging by the gift
of wood-shavings and pale grasses
she had picked and twisted
into a bouquet that lingered on my table.

6. The Dog Fox

Simplify! Simplify!

Which I have already done,
and now do again as a dog fox tiptoes up to my window
at the beginning of Spring
and stares long enough with his glass eyes
to see through me,
or hard enough at least to raise this question:

What am I doing here?

It was the same with the woodchuck
who forgot his wildness
and came to hand
surrendering the secret of his colouring underneath
(more purely brown),

or the garden toad
when I lifted him to my ear
for the enchantment of his faint, chicken-like musical croak,

or the common toad
for a better sight of his golden-coppery iris,

or the turtle dove
with his breast feathers like wind on water.

What am I doing here more than looking –
which I would stop
only to help things through their vanishing,
or thought to learn how best to leave these woods
is why I came to them at first.

7. Cobwebs

Because I had already chosen to bring them with me

along with the hawk who would not leave her nest,

and the snapping turtle whose head is big as a child
but terrible as a crocodile,

and the owl who turned to stone

when I paddled under the hemlock bank,

and the baskets of wild cranberry and huckleberry,

I crept out this morning to see the gossamer webs
extending from my clear ground
towards a stand of black willows
they had completely covered up
with lines in parallel,
not taut,
but curving downwards in the middle,
like the rigging of tall ships
that swoops from mast to mast,
as if a thousand nations had collected under bare poles
but were going nowhere
and content with that.

8. The River

Although I have heard
or could not help myself imagining
in quieter times
the railway with its clink and flutter,
not to mention the lanes and highways,
I always planned to leave these woods
by following the river as I came.

Today
the geese that rise to see me off
will also take its course
but only roughly,
cutting short the twists and turns.

I confine myself
and choose the slow meander of the current,

the long reflections of the trees,

the trees themselves –
beech and pine and conifer –

the echoes which,
as they die out behind me,
sound like water running backwards to its source,
and therefore in good time
return me where I am,
to start again.

AUTHOR'S NOTE: The narrator of 'A Meeting of Minds . . .' takes himself into the wilderness and solitude, where he speaks with and in some respects becomes Thoreau. To suggest this blending, I've wound my own words around others taken from Thoreau's *Journals*.

CHASING WOLVES
IN THE
AMERICAN WEST

Adam Nicolson

Every Monday, the Wolf Telemetry Flight takes off from Springerville, Arizona, soon after eight in the morning. The small, pristine airport – 'Mormon neat', they tell me – is at seven thousand feet above sea level, and the air above it is as pure as milk. Look up and you find yourself gazing into an atmosphere so clean it feels laundered, a limitless blue stretching from here to the edges of space. 'Yep,' says Gary, the pilot from Phoenix, fuel hose in hand, perched over the wing, filling the plane's tanks from a stepladder, 'another lousy Arizona morning.'

The plane is a little Cessna 185, thirty-five years old, with a wolf-finding aerial attached to its belly. I am soon crammed into the back. The leatherette-plastic on the seats is split and scuffed. Gary is in front of me and next to him is Patrick Fitzgerald from the US Fish and Wildlife Service, the federal agency which since 1973 has been charged with bringing wolves back to the American wild.

Patrick is no Western hardman, but a soft, fair-haired, slightly melancholy Arizonan, who this morning is a little flustered. Over the next four hours, using the aerial attached to the plane, he has to find the tiny, endangered population of about a hundred Mexican grey wolves which since 1998 have been released here to breed in the forested and canyoned borderlands of Arizona and New Mexico to the south of us. It is a stressful task, tracking the fifty-odd animals that are fitted with radio collars in an area of more than four million acres, seven thousand square miles, the huge and beautiful province of woodland, mountain and river known as the Blue Range Wolf Recovery Area.

It is the wildest part of the American South-West and, in a way, its most beautiful. Butch Cassidy hid out here, as did Geronimo and his Apaches, and these half-wooded mesas, pale grass meadows and dark canyons are where Aldo Leopold, the godfather of modern American environmental ethics, learned the meaning of wildness and our relationship to it.

Gary guns the engine, radios the young woman in Springerville Tower to say that he has Patrick and 'a ride-along' on board. A prairie dog drops into its burrow beside the runway as we pass and without fuss, as easily as a dinghy slipping its moorings on a quayside, we lift and bounce into the polished, radiant blue of the Arizona sky.

The high range stretches below us in blond slabs between the mountains. Turkey vultures hang like floorboards over the grasslands as we turn east, climbing over the hump of the mountain called Escudilla. There is a dusting of talcum-like snow in Escudilla's creases and the aspens on its western flank are cold and leafless. Spring has yet to arrive up there. To the east the ridges of the Blue Range are lined out one after another, the mountains dark, soaked in ink, with mist still lying in the valleys between them. Beneath us is a mosaic of open and closed, shelter and vista, the grey-green of the dry woodlands and the lion-skin of the high altitude grass.

As we come off the back of Escudilla, low down over its basalt rimrocks, turbulence kicks and buffets at the plane. Patrick adjusts his headphones and talks into the mike pushed up against his lips. 'I've, yes, I've got the alpha. She's down there. I'm not getting the male.' In my headphones, the steady beep of the wolf's signal comes through, a low heartbeat, an electronic hint of life. Gary banks and turns, the wing now pointing straight down at the aspens and we circle above her, the alpha female of the Elk Horn Pack. 'Can you see her?' I say to Patrick. 'No, no,' he says through my headphones, 'you never see them. You just know they are there. She's on the ridge there.' We bank and turn, ever tighter, a thousand-foot circle, Gary hanging the plane above the unseen wolf like a motorcyclist on the wall of death, casually reading out the coordinates of the wolf's position from his GPS. Patrick writes them on his form and the wolf is mapped.

However hard I stare down at her, three or four hundred feet below me, she never appears. The Elk Horn alpha female, like all the other wolves this morning, is hidden among the shadows of the fallen rocks, the old, exhausted winter grasses and the snow scatter of her mountain, her presence reduced to the steady, dematerialized signal in my ear. Nothing less wild, nothing more suggestive of wildness: the electronic trace of a hidden wolf.

We fly on and the Wolf Recovery Area seems limitless below me, a universe of dry, wrinkled, corrugated and folded ridges. Here and there, people have nibbled at the edge, a track, a ranch building, a corral, little mouse-teeth bites into the body of America. The bulk of it seems untouched.

Patrick, control stick in hand, keeps turning the aerial under the plane, patiently locating the precious wolves in the emptiness of their range. He flicks through the radio band, each wolf on a different frequency. The signals can be heard something like eight to ten miles away, faint to begin with, growing louder as we close in on them. Pack by pack we find them: Elk Horn, Fox Mountain, San Mateo, Willow Springs, Canyon Creek, Dark Canyon, Prieto. Again and again, as we come across the wolves below us, Gary throws the plane into its tight circle, the trees cast their sharp diagonal shadows, Patrick notes down the coordinates and I stare at the earth, hoping for a glimpse of pelt or tail.

Occasionally a slick ribbon of highway tarmac appears in the dry woodland. Farm trucks on ranch roads hauling cattle raise plumes of high white dust behind them. In the big, devastated 'burns', where the forest fires have blown through, the trees stand like the stubble on an unshaved chin. All of it is wolf country; nowhere is a wolf to be seen, but they are here, an under-presence, a concealed otherness and a hidden dominance.

Wolves have become the great meaning-vehicles of the American West. For the largely urban ecologists, excited at the idea that America might restore some of the damage done to it in the nineteenth and twentieth centuries, wolves 'belong'. A landscape without wolves is incomplete. They are the 'keystone predators'. Without them the arch of life, in its many trophic levels, is not only broken but insecure. Wolves should be thought of not as parasitic on the animals that sustain them but in some ways the creators and governors of the world they dominate. If the wolves are absent, the arch beneath them bulges and distorts: too many elk and deer, too much uninterrupted browsing on trees, a diminution of bird habitat, no cooling shadows for streams, no beavers, fewer fish. A fractured universe.

Why do wolves have this grip on the modern rewilding imagination? Perhaps because they seem like the best possible vision of how we might be if we were ever thrown back into the wild. Maybe, if we dream right, we might in fact be wolves. Wolves seem as capable, as self-sufficient and as imposing as the best of us. They can live for a week without eating. They can travel twenty miles without breaking stride. They move with an easy, liquid grace through the roughest country. According to the American naturalist Barry Lopez, the Bella Coola Indians thought that a great shaman once tried to change all animals into men but the only things he succeeded in making human were the eyes of the wolf. They have killed people. They certainly kill dogs. In one Alaskan winter they stripped nearly all the dogs out of a village, leaving only the collars to be found by the owners in the morning. They kill coyotes and leave them splayed on prominent paths, uneaten, surrounded by wolf scat, the executed victims laid out for anyone to see.

It is a rough life. Wolves can be fatally injured by a kick from an elk they are pursuing. Many wolves, when found dead, have fractured and mended skulls or broken ribs that have re-fused in life. They live in families, remaining loyal to their sex partners and to their parents. The young, from a succession of litters, hunt with their parents. At least half of all wolf pups die from natural causes in their first year of life but the greatest cause of adult wolf death, apart from human beings, is other wolves. If a pup is severely wounded, parents can kill and eat it. They sing and play together; they grieve aloud; they learn and change; they act by decision as much as by instinct. They communicate over many miles of wilderness by howling, conveying not only their presence but their intentions. If you want to distinguish wolf tracks from dog tracks, you must look for a sense of purpose, not the dog's haphazard wavering after a whim or a scent, but a steady fast padding down the trail.

There is a form of genetic wisdom in wolf behaviour. At two years old, the young adults can choose to stay or go. Some remain with their parental pack; others, both male and female, disperse, looking for unclaimed land and an unclaimed mate. Because breeding within any pack is suppressed to the alpha pair, and because each pack fiercely defends its territory and kills strange wolves, there are never too many wolves in a given stretch of country.

These strategies, which regulate the numbers of wolves, and therefore prey, do not destroy the resource on which the wolves rely. Looking down on the territories of these packs, each covering about 150 or 200 square miles, not that different in size from the cattle ranches which overlie them, I couldn't help but think of them as little fiefdoms, the great estates of the wolf-earls, alive with questions of dominance, rivalry, calculation, loyalty and struggle, an ancient, co-present, parallel world to our own.

We turn west, back over the state line into Arizona. Patrick picks up the alpha female of the Rim Pack, and we continue into the territory of the Tsay-O-Ah Pack, an Apache name. He has done well, finding nearly all the wolves. Just the Tsay-O-Ah and a couple of others still to locate. He is running through the frequencies on his receiver when suddenly and quietly he says, 'We are in trouble here.' A sound I haven't heard before, a quickened beep, is coming through the headphones. It is twice as fast as the note I have been hearing all morning. It sounds like an engaged tone on a landline. 'That is a mortality signal,' Patrick says. 'If a wolf hasn't moved or breathed for twenty minutes, that's the signal we get.'

We circle. Unseen, somewhere below us, at the foot of a burnt cliff, a wolf lies dead. The three of us stare down at the earth. There is a weed-clotted lake below the grey bluff, and a dirt track. 'That's a road running right into the edge of the lake,' Gary says. The implication is clear. This is one of the very remote places where wolves and people might meet in the vast expanse of the wild. It is the sort of place in which a wolf could be shot and no one would ever know who did it. While Patrick texts the Field Office in Alpine, the mortality tone beeps on in the headphones, an insistent anti-heartbeat, and I feel, to my own surprise, a sudden sense of loss over that death hundreds of feet below us, an animal killed not because it was a real threat, nor because it was wanted for its meat or skin, but almost certainly because of its metaphor, because it was unwanted in the rancher's world.

The cellphone signal was patchy and as Gary climbed to improve it, Patrick texted the map coordinates to the federal wildlife crime agency. 'It's a crime scene until otherwise known,' he said. As I sat in the back of the plane that morning, I could think only that this landscape was coloured by a conflict of inheritances and a clash of nostalgias. The wolf advocates might long for a return to the Pleistocene, to the restoration of a complete spectrum of life as it was in America, before the first hunters decimated the megafauna of the continent, a prelapsarian wholeness. But the ranchers who see this land as theirs can think back to another version of the past, the time of their grandparents and great-grandparents coming to the West, making their lives out here in this beautiful, difficult wilderness, leaving their names and experiences – Raw Meat Canyon, Me Own Hill, Pancake Draw – all over the map. They cannot understand why that history, and that belief in themselves, should be threatened by people from the cities who know nothing of what the rancher is or what he needs, and who despise the little they might understand. Why should priority in this place be given to wolves when it could be given to the people who work it? What is better about wildness than the presence of cowboys and their cattle in the wide-open range with the blue mountains on the horizon? That is what the death signal of the wolf below us meant: the serene landscape of my golden morning was nothing of the kind. Below us was a battlefield of competing griefs.

Back on the ground at Springerville, Patrick told me he was doing this work 'so we can fix what we screwed up in the first place. It wasn't our place to kill them. They should be here. This is their place.' That question – just whose place this is – sits at the heart of the wolf agony now convulsing the American West. For the ranchers, the people trying to make their living on this land, wolves are the symbol not of redemption but of an alien government, an urban-tax-funded, federally directed war on state rights, a war on everything the ranchers love and treasure.

The history is not a long one. Much of the wolves' natural prey was exterminated in the nineteenth century. White America brought in millions of cattle to consume the apparently limitless grass. The wolves inevitably preyed on those cattle and just as inevitably the American government, first with bounties to hunters and then with the more effective strychnine, got rid of them. The destruction was essentially commercial, part of the same movement that built the railways, removed the bison, turned the bison bones into fertilizer and invented the refrigerated boxcars in which the beef could be shipped back east. Through the late nineteenth and early twentieth centuries, wolves were exterminated in the whole of the United States except Alaska and a small sliver of Minnesota, with the explicit purpose of making the country safe for cows.

The counter-movement to that emasculation of the wild has its roots just as deep in the nineteenth century. From Henry David Thoreau on through John Muir, the early-twentieth-century animal advocates of the American Society of Mammalogists and Aldo Leopold – the first man to understand that wolves might be capable of regulating their environment – the cult of wilderness spread its tendrils through American society. At its heart was a view of nature as a resource for the nation which went beyond material use: logging, mining, quarrying, damming and grazing were all very well, but the vast space of America surely deserved more.

That idea has shaped much of the American West, partly because it is a difficult place in which to make a living. Civilization struggles here. The sheer poverty of much of the high, dry land west of the Great Plains meant that the pattern of homesteading which had worked on the prairie was unsustainable. No family could survive on 160 acres of desiccated New Mexico. As a result, and under the umbrella of the great federal landowning institutions of the early twentieth century – the National Park Service, the Bureau of Land Management, the Forest Service and the Fish and Wildlife Service – fully one quarter of all American land, 620 million acres, much of it in the West, remains unclaimed and unallocated to individual owners, still today in government ownership. It is one of the great unspoken facts of America that the land of the free largely belongs to the state.

The ranches on which the cowmen run their cattle usually consist of a small patch of privately owned land, perhaps forty or fifty acres, to which vast extents of land are attached as 'allotments', on which the rancher for a small sum is allowed to graze his cattle. This question of ownership is central to the wolf agony because both sides of the question think the public lands, as the environmentalists call them, or the federal lands, as the ranchers call them, are theirs to do with as they wish.

The 1960s and early 70s saw a surge of legislation in which the United States discovered its ability to attend to the well-being of nature. The Wilderness Act, the Clean Air Act, the National Environmental Policy Act, the revision of the Federal Insecticide, Fungicide, and Rodenticide Act, the Marine Mammal Protection Act and finally the Endangered Species Act of 1973 brought about a deep change in the American relationship to the wild.

This shift in federal attitude – it is one wing of the great liberal moment of the mid-twentieth century – meant that the ranchers, from being the heroes of the story of the American West, became its villains. Among the eco-experts, cattle became acknowledged as the agents of ruin. Euro-Americans and their cows – largely British breeds – had arrived in the drylands of the South-West with the sort of expectations they had brought from Europe to the Atlantic seaboard of America: resilient soils and an adaptive environment which could survive the onslaught of a million bovine mouths. But grazing in the dry states inevitably meant overgrazing. Overgrazing meant the destruction of the thin biotic crust which protected and bound the dusty land. The soils began to pour down the river courses which cut deep arroyos into the range. Inedible sage, mesquite and creosote bushes colonized vast areas of what had been open country where the grass had brushed up against the horses' bellies. Cowboys, cows, no wolves and too many deer and elk added up to ecological disaster.

'One of the penalties of an ecological education,' Aldo Leopold wrote, 'is that one lives alone in a world of wounds. Much of the damage inflicted on land is invisible to laymen. An ecologist . . . must be the doctor who sees the marks of death in a community that believes itself well and does not want to be told otherwise.' Uncontrolled grazing, the beautiful Western sight of a cowman with his cattle on the range, could destroy a whole life system; only predators could keep those mouths in check. That is the point of Aldo Leopold's most famous book: 'The cowman who cleans his range of wolves,' he wrote in *A Sand County Almanac*, 'has not learned to think like a mountain. Hence we have dust bowls and rivers washing the future into the sea.'

The Endangered Species Act was intended not only 'to provide a program for the conservation of such endangered species and threatened species' but 'to provide a means whereby the ecosystems upon which endangered species and threatened species depend may be conserved'. Its target was the recreation of a better America and once the Act was passed, the United States government was under a legal obligation to restore the wolves and other now-rare animals that had been destroyed over the previous 150 years.

That Act was signed by, of all people, Richard Nixon, who thought environmentalists were 'hopeless softheads' but was keen to acquire the new tranche of wild-aware voters that had been brought in by the lowering of the voting age in 1971 to eighteen. Apparently unconscious of any long-term consequences of what he was doing, he set in motion the long battle between the two parts of the American soul – pro-wolf, anti-wolf, anti-cow, pro-cow, urban greenery versus rural cowboyism, liberal against conservative, wild against civilized, federal power in Washington against the power of individual states – which has raged ever since, and of which the dead Tsay-O-Ah wolf was only the latest, pitiable victim. Only in America could the phrase 'creeping wilderness' come to seem equivalent to 'over-government', but since 1973 that is how things have stood.

A few days later, deep in the country over which I had flown, I am sitting in the kitchen of Bill and Bettye Powell at Sand Flat Ranch outside Aragon, in Catron County, New Mexico. I've turned up unannounced, wanting to ask them about the little building at the corner of their track where it meets the main road down to Reserve, New Mexico. It is a wooden anti-wolf shelter designed for children who need to wait for the school bus without being eaten by the wolves around them. You can find shelters like this here and there dotted around Catron County, neat structures, with benches inside, wire mesh covering the openings and a bolt, on the inside of the door, unreachable by any wolf, so that the children can lock themselves in.

The Powells' buildings at Sand Flat Ranch are a few miles up the dusty tree-lined road, up in the big sun-bleached and open wood pasture of Catron County. Bill Powell came out to meet me as I drove in, smiling, snaggle-toothed, blue-eyed, telling his dogs to be quiet, the stubble on his cheeks greying on his jowls, his work shirt worn at the collar.

'Oh that thing,' he said, when I asked about the wolf shelter. 'That's what they call "a statement".' He looked at me. 'The school put it there. I think the county paid for them. And no,' laughing, 'we certainly never did use it. Who would put their kids down there and leave them there anyway? We always waited for the bus to come. And the bus driver waited for us if we weren't there. It was just . . . just a show. Do you want a hamburger?'

His wife Bettye and their sixteen-year-old son Brock are having lunch in the kitchen. She looks drawn. She shows me a letter she had written to Susana Martínez, the young Republican governor of New Mexico. The governor – the Latino Sarah Palin, she has been called – likes nothing about the wolves and has withdrawn any New Mexico involvement with the recovery programme.

'Dear Governor Martínez,' Bettye had written,

> Our bright Monday morning turns to one of dread as we hear the drone of an airplane as it circles above us. What that sound has come to mean to us is that there is a wolf pack on our ranch.
>
> Not a pleasant way to start the week, but with the weekly flights to locate the wolves, more common than one would suppose.
>
> It unnerves me to think about calving season and spring. Usually my favorite time – the miracle of birth itself, of those little just-born, stiff-legged calves nestling up to their lowing mothers – that's one of the loves of ranching. Spring . . . rebirth . . . hope. Yet I look to it with a feeling of utter desolation.

The two of them sitting at the table seemed drained. I see for the first time just how bloodshot Bill's eyes are. Bettye's face is creased and wrinkled around her eyes. Biologists speak casually and intriguingly of 'the ecology of fear' in relationship to wolves. If the ungulates – the deer and the elk – know there are wolves in the area, they behave quite differently: watchful, anxious, choosing not to browse in places from which escape is difficult, where fallen rocks or steep stream valleys might slow them down as they try to run. And that difference in behaviour creates what is called 'a trophic cascade', a ripple effect travelling down and out through the many different participants in an ecosystem, from the unbrowsed streamside willows or cottonwoods, to the invertebrates living in the trees, or the birds that might like to nest in them, and even the forms taken by the streams themselves in a less tightly grazed country. In that way, wolves shape their world. Some eco-theorists have linked this 'ecology of fear' to what they also call the 'geography of hope', the possibility that in wildness, as Thoreau wrote in his famous essay 'Walking', 'is the preservation of the world'. Fear makes for a redeemed ecology, one into which the reality of violent death injects a kind of health and vigour.

Here, now, in the Powells' kitchen, that way of thinking looked sick. I suddenly saw what the 'ecology of fear' might actually mean for a family attempting to ranch these dry acres. Bill and Bettye have been here for eleven years. Only forty acres are their own. The other forty thousand they have as an allotment from the Bureau of Land Management and on that federal land they are, for a small monthly payment, allowed to run three hundred head of cattle.

'Ranching is a disease,' Bill said, smiling at me, 'if you ever catch the bug. It's kind of like a guy inherited a million dollars. "What are you goin' to do?" they asked him. "I am going to ranch until I run out of money." You've got a couple of million dollars of assets but your income is below poverty level.' In fact, in their worst years they have been living off $18,000 a year. 'When you lose $11 to $20,000 of livestock a year, you can't take many vacations,' Bill said.

'Those aren't confirmed kills, Bill,' Bettye said. 'You have to have bruising in the tissue beneath the skin to be a confirmed kill.'

'That's true,' Bill said, 'but I think we've been lied to a lot. People have said many things to us which we don't think are true.'

Uncertainty stains every corner of their lives. 2010 was when their bad time with 'the wooves' began – Bill says the word without the l. 'That was the first year we really had trouble. A pack was on us – killing calves. It was the San Mateo Pack. We think we lost eighteen calves due to the wooves. But we only had one confirmed kill and one confirmed attack.'

'They were tore up,' Bettye said, 'chewed up, big hunks ripped out of their hams, their hind ends.'

'Big slashes on their sides,' Brock, their son, said.

His mother looked across at him. 'One calf was chewed up pretty bad at the hip,' she said. 'We babied it and doctored it and two months later it was well enough to put out. And two days later it was a kill.'

Neighbours of theirs have given up, either no longer stocking their allotments or putting their places up for sale. The central difficulty is that although ranchers are compensated for 'depredations' by wolves that can be proved, there can be no compensation for the underlying and pervasive sense of anxiety which wolves have brought into their lives. The Powells are now part of 'the ecology of fear', whether they like it or not.

'The first year we didn't know we had a pack,' Bettye said. 'We lost about ten first-calf heifers. If one starts running, they all take off.'

'Yuh,' Bill said. 'They had all been run down. Something was running and exhausting them. That time of year and condition, it doesn't take much. It's an iffy thing. You don't know anything. It's really hard to prove. You suspect them. Baby calves disappear. Wooves clean it all up and you don't have anything to prove anything with. It's really hard to sit here and say the wooves are the whole cause of the trouble. We've had drought. We had the big Wallow forest fire and we had two cows die of respiratory complications because of the smoke from that fire. But the wooves are just that one thing extra.'

We sat there in silence for a second. 'I'm at a point where I am not hireable in the workforce,' Bill said. 'I'm fifty-two now. We've not been making a whole lot of money. I don't know what else I could do.'

I wondered if things might be a little different for the next generation. One or two ranchers have been using the wolves to bring in holidaymakers, wolf-watching. But so far anyway, the only wolf benefit this family is getting is from Brock working as a range-rider, on his horse every day, riding with the cattle, paid $500 a month by an ecological group called the Defenders of Wildlife, as part of a programme to encourage coexistence between ranching families and the wolves on their land. 'Just to keep the wolves away, just by being there, by being a presence. We've got three packs within ten miles of here. San Mateo, Fox Mountain and Willow. That's sixteen wolves. One day I was out there I saw eleven in one day.'

'Yes,' Bettye said, 'and what about when you were younger, Brock?' She pointed out of the kitchen window at the dusty road you can see making its way over the pale grasses for half a mile or more.

'I saw two of them coming down that road to our gate,' Brock said. 'I used to be everywhere all over our land, but not after that.'

'He built himself a spear,' his mother said, 'and went about with me when I was hanging up the washing. Is that what you want for your children? To be defending their mothers when they are out at the washing line?'

I spent four days in the Blue Range Wolf Recovery Area with the man who fought for it, created it, populated it with wolves and whose career in the end was destroyed by it.

Dave Parsons does, in some ways, look like a wolf. He has a grizzled grey beard, and his whole presence is slight, honed and precise. Everything about the man is alert and he is one of the most observant men I have ever met, able to summon wild creatures from the shadows: a herd of elk; a group of pronghorns a mile away on the big open pastures; in an ancient riverside walnut tree, a pair of black hawks, all gloss, just in from their winter in Mexico; wild, white-eyed blackbirds; red-tailed hawks, horned larks and western bluebirds and cliff swallows. One day, when we were fifty miles from the nearest hardtop road, he brought me to a small, dry canyon. A prairie falcon was nesting in its cliffs. It flew over and across us for half an hour in a display of wild beauty, its wings flecked brown and khaki, with the sunlight shining through its primaries so that the whole bird seemed fringed with light. 'I don't get into that sappy woo-woo stuff,' he said to me after a day or two out in the recovery area, 'but if there is one thing

I am proud of in my life it's that we brought wolves back to this place.'

His story is an emblem of the contested wild. He is the son of an Iowa prairie farmer, who like his brothers scratched around the farm with a gun as a boy, but they all knew in the 1960s that the days of the family farm were ending. He became a biologist and joined the US Fish and Wildlife Service in 1973, just after the Endangered Species Act had been passed. In those optimistic years, the agency was starting to surf the wolf wave. The grey wolf of the northern Rockies and the Texas grey wolf were both listed as endangered that year and the Mexican grey wolf, a much smaller subspecies whose historic range reached from southern New Mexico and Arizona across the border into Mexico itself, joined them in 1976.

The wheels of rewilding turn slowly. In the early 1980s, the 2.2 million acres of Yellowstone National Park, where there were no cattle or ranchers and no hunting was allowed, was identified as a prime candidate for wolf reintroductions. But the political dimensions of the idea were already becoming clear. The Wyoming ranchers on the borders of the park, led by a Republican representative from Wyoming, a certain Richard B. Cheney, were fiercely against reintroduction. Predictions were made that children would be killed and under the Republican presidencies of Reagan and the first George Bush, the Fish and Wildlife Service dragged its feet. Green groups started suing the agency for failing to do its duty under the Act, but only in 1995, well into the Clinton presidency, were wolves from Canada released in Yellowstone, a grand political statement of Democratic liberty for animals and doing the right thing by the natural world.

Wolves boomed in and around Yellowstone. They changed the whole environment there, climbing to nine hundred individuals by 2005, stoking the park's economy and allowing some 350,000 tourists a year to catch a glimpse of wolves in the wild. Wolves were also doing well in the wildlands west of the Great Lakes but things would never be so easy in the cattle-filled, rancher-rich and politically agonized conditions of Arizona and New Mexico, where there was no national park, no ban on hunting and a huge number of cows.

The little Mexican grey wolf had long been exterminated in the United States and was on the verge of extinction in Mexico. Four individuals were in captivity in the US and Mexico, and in 1978–80 the Fish and Wildlife Service hired a trapper to capture five more in Mexico. These nine animals (of which only seven turned out to be fertile) represented the frighteningly thin genetic thread from which hung the future of the Mexican wolf.

An anxious and rapid breeding programme was begun in recovery centres in America and Mexico, to cross these different strains, to get some hybrid vigour into the population and to preserve as wide a genetic inheritance as they could. Because the Reagan administration had an inbuilt liking for the cowboy and his liberty-imagery, and had little sympathy for wolf reintroductions, federal money and encouragement were both short throughout the eighties. When Parsons was appointed by the Fish and Wildlife Service in October 1990 to be the Mexican wolf recovery coordinator, little had happened. The Reagan government had given individual states control over wolf releases on their territory and environmentalists were again suing the Fish and Wildlife Service to do its duty.

It was a tangle of different political authorities, state-based and federal, all operating in the gravitational fields of vast cultural and symbolic forces. Texas refused to have any wolves, and New Mexico suggested the virtually sterile White Sands missile testing range. Arizona came up with a multiplicity of suggestions, but, on the basis of a scientific analysis of all sites, Parsons knew there could only be one place. What is now the Blue Range Wolf Recovery Area was his chosen country, 4.3 million acres of grasslands, scattered piñon pine, oak and juniper woods, with tall and stately ponderosa pine and mixed conifer forests above that, spread across the Arizona–New Mexico border. The headwaters of the Gila River run through here in deep and shady canyons, filled with elk and deer, much of it ungrazed by cattle. It is a kind of paradise and a place that Parsons loved.

Most of this huge area, the size of five or six English counties, was designated as National Forest, 750,000 acres of it as 'wilderness'. No machinery or construction of any kind can be used there, no cars, no trucks, no chainsaws, no bicycles, no hang-gliders. No road can be built in it. Backpacking in this Gila Wilderness in 1990, Parsons promised himself that in ten years' time he would return and lie there at night, listening to the howling of the wolves he had brought back to America. No place could be better suited to them.

Nothing was going to be easy. New Mexico state officials and high-ups in the federal Fish and Wildlife Service wanted wolves confined to White Sands. Ranchers and their political advocates were massing on the sidelines. Parsons was already receiving threats of violence. Only in 1997, by getting through, somehow – and he still does not quite understand how – to Bruce Babbitt, Clinton's Secretary of the Interior, did Parsons finally get the decision he wanted. The Blue Range was to be the wolf recovery area, wolves to be released only on the Arizona side but able to wander into the New Mexico side.

His eyes shine when he tells this story. But his superiors in the Fish and Wildlife Service were furious that a low-down coordinator had hijacked the process and convinced Clinton's cabinet he was right and they were wrong. It was a triumph, as Parsons saw it, of science – the best place for wolves – and law – the obligation to do right by the wolves – over a small, rancher-dominated interest group.

On 29 March 1998, in the middle of a blizzard, eleven wolves in three packs were released into the Blue Range. Three of them were pregnant females, ready to start 'denning', to give birth to pups which would then know nothing but the wild.

Over that spring and summer the long catastrophe began to unfold. By November five of the eleven wolves had been shot dead. Two more were missing. In an atmosphere of crisis and failure, the remaining animals were captured and brought back into protective custody, largely because they were thought to be at risk from the enraged rancher population and their allies.

Nevertheless, Parsons was committed to the path and releases continued. He had the deep pleasure of re-releasing wolves into the Gila Wilderness, carried in boxes strapped to the back of mules, and of waiting, camping in the silence of that giant emptiness, for the moment they would howl on the hillsides around him. But even as the wolves were released, the illegal killings continued. In the fifteen years since 1998, there have been ninety-two Mexican grey wolf deaths in the wild, forty-seven of them from illegal shooting and twenty-eight shootings by the wildlife authorities after wolves had been preying on cattle or becoming a nuisance. Only four people have been prosecuted and the wolf population has not recovered with anything like the vigour Parsons and his colleagues hoped for. The protected and almost zoo-like circumstances of Yellowstone could not be replicated here.

In the autumn of 1999, it was suggested, neutrally enough, that Parsons might go for early retirement from the Fish and Wildlife Service. It was something many officials of the agency did, taking their pension and getting rehired by the agency at no more than a top-up salary. It saved the government money and Parsons was happy to do it. In the two weeks between his 'retirement' and his beginning to work on wolf recovery again, he went backpacking in the Gila.

On his return to Albuquerque, the phone call asking him to return to his post never came. The regional director of the Fish and Wildlife Service refused to rehire him. Nor was he allowed to volunteer for the programme. He says now that it was 'sabotage', that he was 'deceived', that it was 'a kick in the stomach', that the agency, now firmly in the grip of rancher politics, wanted to destroy the wolf reintroduction programme, that he was too adamant a wolf advocate to be the coordinator of something which needed more sensitivity to the needs of the ranching community, that he was 'politically naive'. Science and the law were on his side, but politics was not and he was forced to leave the service.

Since then, the wolf programme has stumbled along a troubled and deeply compromised path. By early 2000, four packs had been recaptured and were confined to pens. The number of wolves out in the wild was scarcely growing. Even though the biologists were insistent that the full genetic range of wolves should be put out into the wild as soon as possible, any sense of scientific urgency in the agency evaporated in the face of opposition. As we lay one afternoon on the edge of a stretch of grassland watching a herd of elk grazing on the distant, straw-yellow pasture, Parsons said to me, 'The only reason these wolves have not done as well as they should have is because the agency has lacked the balls to blow through the political pressure to do the right thing.'

It has been a desperate story. At meetings in the Recovery Area, violence has bubbled up to the surface. Rancher families have talked of living 'under siege from extreme environmentalism' and 'cultural genocide'. A rancher has pointed at the Fish and Wildlife Service biologist Wendy Brown (once Dave Parsons's deputy) and yelled, 'Wendy Brown, when one of these children dies up here because of these wolves, how are you going to feel?' At another meeting the same man told Parsons, 'I hate your fucking ass,' before punching a local reporter in the stomach.

The Fish and Wildlife Service has back-pedalled for years, surrendering power to the local fish and game authorities, setting up a three-strikes rule by which any wolf that was found to have attacked cattle three times should be permanently removed from the wild either by being shot or permanently caged elsewhere, however valuable that wolf might be to the dwindling genetic resource of the wolf population. The number of Mexican grey wolves in the wild actually declined between 2003 and 2009, sinking to a low of forty-two. Ranchers were found to be deliberately leaving carcasses out on the range so that wolves might get used to eating beef rather than deer or elk, encouraging them to make their three fatal strikes. Reports made by nationally respected scientists, recommending that there should be three populations of Mexican grey wolves of at least two hundred wolves per population, in widely separated areas of the South-West, have been ignored and sidelined for years. Scientific papers commissioned by the Fish and Wildlife Service itself have been chaotically organized and found to be intellectually wanting. In other parts of the United States wolf populations have thrived to the point where they are no longer considered endangered. Here in the South-West, despite the $28 million spent on their recovery, Mexican grey wolves continue to creep along the margins of viability, genetically depleted, under attack physically and politically, scarcely supported by the government agency whose legal obligation it is to guarantee their future. It has been a long and painful shambles. The universal scientific opinion is that a new set of regulations due to be introduced later this year will do little to change the vulnerability of the population. Nothing is less wild than the American wild and the Mexican grey wolf recovery programme is evidence of that.

One night, camping with Dave Parsons on the very edge of the Gila Wilderness, at a high, beautiful half-wooded pasture called Cooney Prairie, I lay out in the cold with a blanket over my sleeping bag, a woolly hat on my head, the frost prickling on the skin of my face and my nose pointing resolutely at the stars. I have never seen night skies like this. The spaces between the stars I know from home are filled here with a kind of star-rubbish, a star-smear, as if someone had forgotten to sweep up the floor of the night sky. No one would ever design a night sky like this. In among them all, the big disc of Jupiter shone so brightly that if I held one hand in front of the other, it cast a blue shadow across my skin. I remembered as I lay there that Newton, when trying to isolate the colours of light, and finding the sun too fat a source, so that his results weren't sharp, was able one night in Cambridge to use Jupiter as his point source. And so, I thought, lying there at eight thousand feet, perhaps this unmediated profligacy of the universe was what men used to see. And that one of the purposes of wilderness might be to take you back to how things were, not to something simple but to something complex, the too-much of the world, the net of intricacy we would see and know if the reductions and definitions of modernity did not prevent us.

I slept and every now and then woke to find the constellations turned a few degrees above me, circling through the branches of the pines, an angular rotation, like the second hand of a station clock, tick-tocking across the night sky. Soon after one in the morning, in a still and silent part of the night, a gang of coyotes not far away started yapping and snapping at each other, or so I thought, like a crowd of kids, a playground squabble in the high country savannah, rising and falling in their tussles and struggles. I have sat in bird colonies in Scotland on still summer nights and heard the seabirds rumbling and yawing at each other like this, the everyday noise of lives accommodating other lives, shuffling and grumbling for room, comfort or acceptance.

But I was wrong. The coyotes weren't yapping at each other. About twenty minutes after they had begun, the cause of their anxiety made itself heard, something quite different, low, adult, magisterial. I thought at first it was the wind which earlier in the evening had blown through the ponderosa pines but the note began to modulate, a broken fall and I heard it for what it was. The howl of this wolf, lasting maybe forty-five seconds, about fifty yards from where I was lying, was a warning, not a proclamation. It was a slow single voice, proprietorial, low then lower, asserting its dominance over the coyotes in the night, all the power, and you could say the humanity, of it in the dropping of the pitch, more animate than the wind could ever be, more *meant*, a statement from the bass line of the world. Then it was gone, the silence as resonant as the voice had been. De-extinction at night, with the light of Jupiter shining through the trees.

The next morning we went looking for the tracks. Dave found them: the wolf had padded down the dirt road that ran past the stand of trees we had been sleeping in. The wolf was lame, only putting three of its feet down as it made its way across country, but each footprint was huge, nearly five inches by four, the size of a child's hand. 'I'm so pleased you heard that,' Dave said. 'Really, I couldn't be more pleased. The one thing I know I can say is that I have made this the place where the wolves can howl.'

Can you step beyond all the grief and discontent of this story, to think in any way as Leopold or Thoreau required us to think about our relationship to the wild? I somehow doubt it. I remember a local environmentalist telling me how a rancher, hating his love of wilderness, had trapped his cat, skinned it and displayed it in the shop down the road in Alpine, Arizona, for a laugh. I think of Bettye Powell's sad and exhausted eyes. I think of the hurt buried in Parsons himself at the memory of his being cheated out of his job and his purpose, all the dignity of his belief in science and law and the virtues of the natural world trashed by a compromise with some rather dirty symbol-politics. And I think of Bill Powell asking me to come back one day and to ride out with him on the range just so I could see what it was like to be him.

Gary Snyder wrote these beautiful lines, a hymn to humility:

> As the crickets' soft autumn hum
> is to us
> so are we to the trees
> as are they
> to the rocks and the hills.

That is a kind of trophic cascade, or at least a modesty cascade through the trophic levels of creation. But can anyone really live according to that? Are our present difficulties and pains, our need to negotiate our lives, not too urgent for that kind of wisdom? Aldo Leopold may have urged Americans 'to think like a mountain'. But I can't imagine how America ever could. ∎

MITAKUYE OYASIN

Aaron Huey

On 29 December 1890, the US 7th Cavalry surrounded a Sioux encampment at Wounded Knee Creek in South Dakota and massacred Chief Spotted Elk and three hundred prisoners of war. After the so-called battle, some twenty Congressional Medals of Honor were awarded.

Today the Oglala Lakota live in the shadow of Wounded Knee on the Pine Ridge Indian Reservation.

I started photographing on Pine Ridge in 2005 as part of a story about poverty in America. In the beginning, it was all just statistics: a 90 per cent unemployment rate, a 70 per cent school dropout rate and a male life expectancy of forty-seven years. Over time, it became clear to me that these statistics came from a deep historical wound. And then my photographs of Pine Ridge became a story about a prisoner -of-war camp, a story about genocide, a story about stolen lands.

Years after beginning this project, the story and my relationships on the reservation are more complex than ever. The story has evolved to be about my family, about the people who call me brother and nephew and uncle.

'Mitakuye Oyasin', translated into English, means 'All my relations'. The Oglala Lakota say this at the beginning and at the end of ceremonies. One of my brothers, Andrew Ironshell, says it means 'a responsibility, almost a call to action, or an acknowledgement that you are a relative to the land, and to the environment and the human beings around you'.

I have stumbled into something sacred on Pine Ridge. I don't know which part is the ceremony. I think, maybe, it is the whole thing. ∎

1. Manderson, South Dakota

2. North of Manderson, South Dakota

3. Stanley Good Voice Elk, a Heyoka, or sacred clown, burning sage to ritually purify his surroundings, Oglala, South Dakota

4. Cody in his bedroom, Manderson, South Dakota

5. Mitchell Crow plays with his dog on what remains of 28,000 pounds of donated used clothes near Loneman, South Dakota. Unclaimed, the rain-soaked handouts go mouldy during the summer.

6. A horseback rider on the Crazy Horse Ride travels from
Chadron, Nebraska to the Crazy Horse camp at Beaver Wall,
to commemorate the life and death of the great Lakota Warrior.

7. Portrait of the Lakota Chief, Red Cloud (1822–1909), with school photo, Manderson, South Dakota

8. A buffalo skull left to dry on a fence post near Oglala, South Dakota, will later be used in the Sun Dance ceremony.

9. The camp of a Native American resistance group in Porcupine, South Dakota, flies the American flag upside down as a symbol of disrespect to the occupying power.

10. Travis Lone Hill, Manderson, South Dakota

11. Three-year-old C.J. Shot bathes among dishes. The Oglala concept of *tiospaye* (unity of the extended family) means that homes are often overcrowded, especially with the severe housing shortage on the reservation. At the time of this photograph, twenty-two people lived in this three-bedroom house in Manderson, South Dakota.

12. Preparation for the Sun Dance, Thunder Lake, South Dakota

13. The White Plume family land near Manderson, South Dakota

14. Powwow in Kyle, South Dakota

15. Grand Entry at the Oglala Nation Powwow, Pine Ridge, South Dakota

16. Badlands near Red Shirt Table, South Dakota

17. Manderson, South Dakota

18. Evergreen, South Dakota

LOOKING FOR MORE?

Subscribe to *Granta* to save up to 29% on the cover price and get free access to the magazine's entire digital archive.

Complete the form overleaf, visit granta.com or call (845)267-3031

US
$48

CANADA
$56

LATIN AMERICA
$68

'Provides enough to satisfy the most rabid appetite for good writing and hard thinking'
– *Washington Post*

GRANTA.COM

GRANTA

THE MAGAZINE OF NEW WRITING

SUBSCRIPTION FORM FOR US, CANADA AND LATIN AMERICA

Yes, I would like to take out a subscription to *Granta*.

GUARANTEE: If I am ever dissatisfied with my *Granta* subscription, I will simply notify you, and you will send me a complete refund or credit my credit card, as applicable, for all un-mailed issues.

YOUR DETAILS

MR / MISS / MRS / DR ....

NAME ....

ADDRESS ....

....

CITY... STATE ....

ZIP CODE .... COUNTRY ....

EMAIL ....

☐ Please check this box if you do not wish to receive special offers from *Granta*

☐ Please check this box if you do not wish to receive offers from organizations selected by *Granta*

YOUR PAYMENT DETAILS

1 year subscription: ☐ US: $48 ☐ Canada: $56 ☐ Latin America: $68

3 year subscription: ☐ US: $120 ☐ Canada: $144 ☐ Latin America: $180

Enclosed is my check for $ _____ made payable to *Granta*.

Please charge my: ☐ Visa ☐ MasterCard ☐ Amex

Card No. ☐☐☐☐☐☐☐☐☐☐☐☐☐☐☐☐

Exp. ☐☐☐☐

Security Code ☐☐☐☐☐

SIGNATURE .... DATE ....

Please mail this order form with your payment instructions to:

Granta Publications
PO Box 359
Congers, NY 10920-0359

Or call 845-267-3031
Or visit GRANTA.COM for details

Source code: BUS128PM

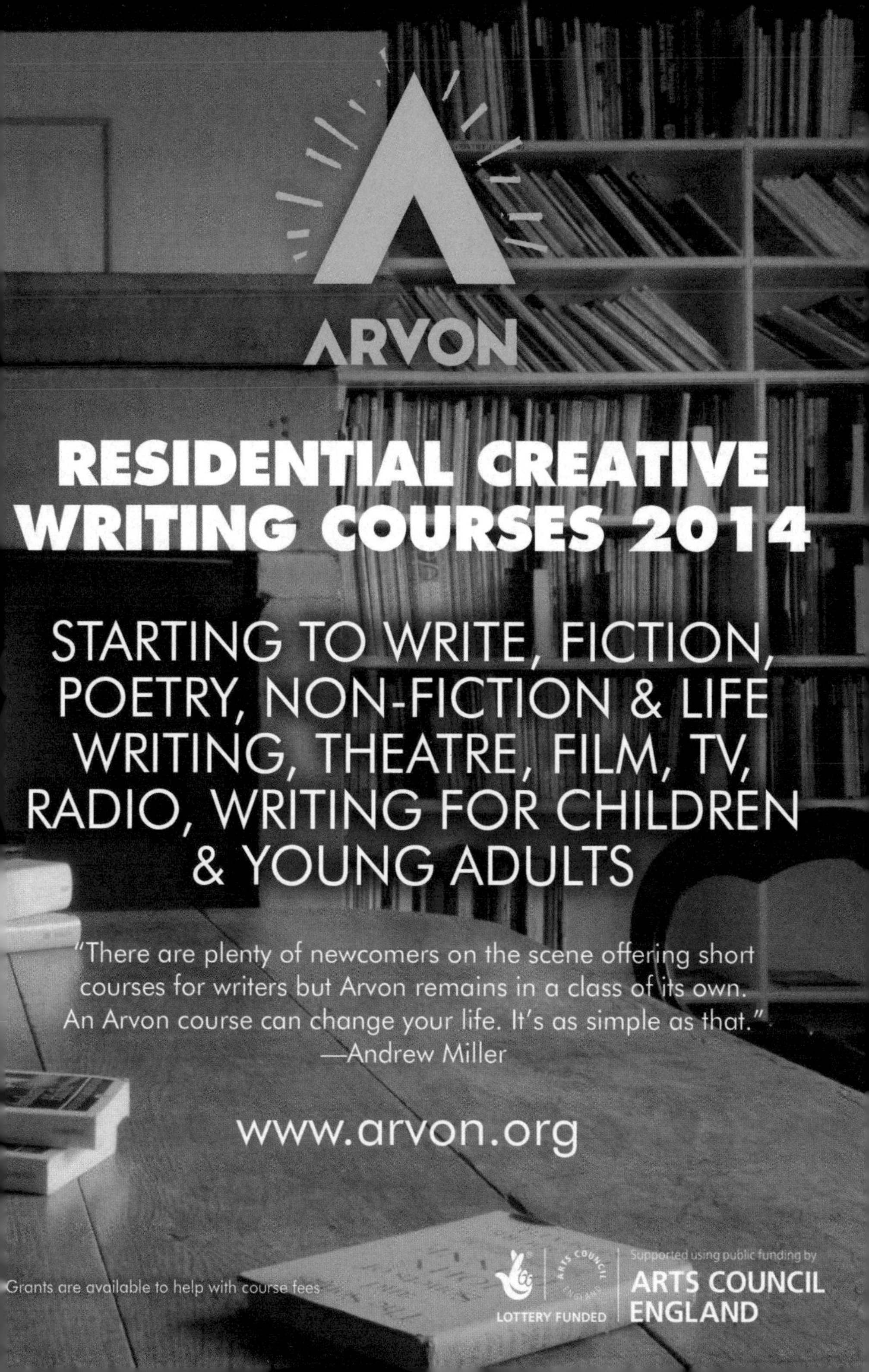
ARVON
RESIDENTIAL CREATIVE WRITING COURSES 2014
STARTING TO WRITE, FICTION, POETRY, NON-FICTION & LIFE WRITING, THEATRE, FILM, TV, RADIO, WRITING FOR CHILDREN & YOUNG ADULTS
"There are plenty of newcomers on the scene offering short courses for writers but Arvon remains in a class of its own. An Arvon course can change your life. It's as simple as that."
—Andrew Miller
www.arvon.org
Grants are available to help with course fees
LOTTERY FUNDED
Supported using public funding by
ARTS COUNCIL ENGLAND

Beyond Sunset

Blue sadness is sweetness cut into strips with scissors and then into little pieces by a knife, it is the sadness of reverie and nostalgia. It may be, for example, the memory of a happiness which is now only a memory, it has receded into a niche that cannot be dusted for it is beyond your reach; distinct and dusty, blue sadness lies in your inability to dust it, it is as unreachable as the sky, it is a fact reflecting the sadness of all facts. Blue sadness is that which you wish to forget, but cannot, as when on a bus one suddenly pictures with absolute clarity a ball of dust in a closet, such an odd, unshareable thought that one blushes, a deep rose spreading over the blue fact of sadness, creating a situation that can only be compared to a temple, which exists, but to visit it one would have to travel two thousand miles on snowshoes and by dog sled, five hundred by horseback and another five hundred by boat, with a thousand by rail.

Gray sadness is the sadness of paper clips and rubber bands, of rain and squirrels and chewing gum, ointments and unguents and movie theatres. Gray sadness is the most common of all sadnesses, it is the sadness of sand in the desert and sand on the beach, the sadness of keys in a pocket, cans on a shelf, hair in a comb, dry-cleaning, and raisins. Gray sadness is beautiful, but not to be confused with the beauty of blue sadness, which is irreplaceable. Sad to say, gray sadness is replaceable, it can be replaced daily, it is the sadness of a melting snowman in a snowstorm.

Pink sadness is the sadness of white anchovies. It is the sadness of deprivation, of going without, of having to swallow when your throat is no bigger than an acupuncture pin, it's the sadness of mushrooms born with heads too big for their body, the sadness of having the sole come off your only pair of shoes, or your favourite pair, it makes no difference, pink sadness cannot be measured by a game-show host, it is the sadness of shame when you have done nothing wrong, pink sadness is not your fault, and though even the littlest twinge may cause it, it is the vast bushy top on the family tree of sadness, whose faraway roots resemble a colossal squid with eyes the size of soccer balls.

Red sadness is the secret one. Red sadness never appears sad, it appears as Nijinsky bolting across the stage in mid-air, it appears in flashes of passion, anger, fear, inspiration and courage, in dark unsellable visions; it is an upside-down penny concealed beneath a tea cosy, the even-tempered and steady-minded are not exempt from it, and a curator once attached this tag to it: *Because of the fragile nature of the pouch no attempt has been made to extract the note.* ■

© STEPHEN SHORE
from *American Surfaces*, 1972
Courtesy of 303 Gallery, New York

GRANDMA
AND ME

Thomas McGuane

My grandmother lost her sight about three years ago, just before she turned ninety, and because it happened gradually, and in the context of so much other debility, she adapted very well. Grandma's love of the outdoors combined with her remarkable lucidity and optimism to keep her cheerful and realistic. And she could get on my ass about as good as she ever could. She was now greatly invested in her sense of smell, so I tried to put fresh flowers around her house while Mrs Devlin, her housekeeper of forty-one years, kept other things in the cottage fresh, including the flow of gossip and the newspaper under Chickie, a thirty-year-old blue-fronted parrot that had bitten me several times. When Grandma goes, Chickie is going into the Disposal.

Grandma did a remarkable job of living in the present, something I'd hoped to learn from her before going broke or even crazier than I already was. I'd been away for over a decade, first as a timekeeper in a palladium mine, then dealing cards, downhill all the way. Three years in a casino left me so fucked up I was speaking in tongues, but Grandma got me back on my feet with pearls of immortal wisdom like, 'Pull yourself together.' And while I waited for her to give me a little walking-around money, a pearl or two would come to me too, like, 'Shit or get off the pot.'

Grandma owned several buildings in the middle of our small town, including the old hotel where I lived. I looked after them, not exactly as a maintenance man – I don't have such trade skills – but more as an overseer, for which Grandma paid me meagrely, justifying her stinginess with the claim that I was bleeding her white. Another building housed an office-supply shop and a preschool, where I was a teaching assistant. That is, a glorified hall monitor for a bunch of dwarfs. I also tended bar two nights a week – the off nights, when tips were scarce, but it was something to do and kept me near the hooch. Grandma had bought the bar, too, back when it was frequented mainly by sheep-herders. Sheep have mostly disappeared from the area since being excluded from the national forest, which they had defoliated better than Agent Orange. I didn't see much point in tending an empty bar, but Grandma required it. It was part of my 'package', she said, and besides she was sure that if we closed it down, it would become a meth lab. Grandma was convinced every empty building housed a meth lab.

The preschool thing was another matter. Mrs Hessler, the teacher, considered me her employee, and I played along with this to keep the frown off that somewhat shapeless face she had crowned with an inappropriate platinum pixie. I regularly fed her made-up news items from imaginary newspapers, and she always bought it. 'Drone Strike on a Strip Club', for example. In return, Mrs Hessler made me wear clothes she supplied and considered kid-friendly; loud leisure suits and sweatpants, odd-lot items that gave me the feeling I was at the end of my rope.

Barring weather or a World Series game, on Sundays I'd pick up a nice little box lunch from Mustang Catering and take Grandma some place that smelled good. I was often in rough shape on Sunday mornings, so a little fresh air helped me dry out in time for work on Monday. We'd have our picnics in fields of sage and lupin, on buffalo grass savannahs north of town, on deep beds of spruce needles and in fields of spring wild flowers. I'd have enough of nature pretty quick, but we stayed until Grandma had had her fill; she told me it was the least I could do and I suppose she's right.

Today's nature jaunt turned out to be one for the ages: we went to a bend in the river near Grandma's and set up our picnic under the oldest of cottonwoods, the eastbound current racing toward us over pale gravel. It smelled wonderful. Once out of the car, I led Grandma with a light touch on the elbow, marvelling at how straight and tall she was, how queenly she looked with her thick white hair carefully piled and secured by Mrs Devlin with a broad tortoiseshell comb. I had just settled Grandma on her folding chair and popped open our box lunch when the corpse floated by. Though face down he seemed formally attired, and the tumult of current at the bend was strong enough to make him ripple from end to end, while his arms seemed lofted in some oddly valedictory way and his hair floated ahead of him. The sunlight sparkling on the water made the picture ghastly.

'Oh!' said Grandma as though she could see it.

'What?'

'That divine smell, of course! I can still smell snow in the river!'

The corpse had rotated in such a way that I could now see the heels of its shoes and the slight ballooning of its suit coat. Just then I remembered that cheap Allegiant flight I'd taken back from Las Vegas. I'd lost so much money, I got drunk on the plane and passed out, and someone scrawled LOSER on my face in eyebrow pencil, though I didn't see it until the men's room at the Helena airport. Was I so far gone I was identifying with a corpse?

'What an awful child you were,' Grandma said. 'Already drinking in the sixth grade. What would have become of you if I hadn't put you in Catholic school? It was your salvation and thank goodness the voodoo wore off in time. It wasn't easy humouring those silly nuns. They never took their hands out of their sleeves the whole time you were there.'

'Uh, Grandma, excuse me but I have to see a man about a horse.' I jogged along the riverbank until I was well out of earshot and, lighting a cigarette, I called the sheriff's office on my cell. I let the dispatcher know who I was and asked if the sheriff or one of the deputies was available. 'I'll check. What's the topic?' The dispatcher's tone let me know how they felt about me at the sheriff's office.

'I'm down on the river and a corpse just went by. Across from the dump. It's going to pass under the Harlowton Bridge in about ten minutes.'

'There's no one here right now. Marvin has a speeder pulled over at the prairie dog town. Maybe he could get there.'

'Next stop after that is Greycliff. Somebody'd have to sit on the bridge all day.'

'Please don't raise your voice. Any distinguishing features?'

'How's "dead" sound to you?'

I went back to find Grandma lifting her face in the direction of the sun and seeming contented. A few cottonwood leaves fluttering in a breath of wind onto the surface of the river revealed the speed of the current. Every so often people floated by on rafts, blue rafts, yellow rafts, their laughter and conversations carried along on the water like a big, happy wake following a corpse.

'Are you ready to eat?' I asked.

'In a bit, unless you're hungry now. It smells different than when we were here in August. I think something happens when the leaves begin to turn, something cidery in the air, and yesterday's rain stays in the trunks of these old trees.' It had rained for about two minutes yesterday. Grandma's got all these sensations dialled in as though she's cramming the entire earth before morting out for good.

I walked down to the river, took off my shoes and socks and rolled up my pant legs. I waded in no more than a few inches when I heard my phone ring. I turned just in time to see Grandma groping for it next to where I'd left the box lunches. Oh, well. I kept wading and noticed three white pelicans standing among the car bodies on the far side of the river. I'd have thought they'd have gone south by now. I dug a few flat stones off the bottom and skipped them toward the middle of the river. I got five skips from a piece of bottle glass before going back to Grandma.

'That was the sheriff's office.'

'Oh?'

'They wanted you to know that it was a jilted groom who jumped into Yankee Jim Canyon on Sunday. What day is today?'

'Wednesday.' Must have averaged a couple miles an hour.

'Why would they think you'd care about a jilted groom jumping into Yankee Jim Canyon?'

'Idle curiosity,' I said sharply.

'And the sheriff was calling just to fill you in? I don't understand one bit of that, not one bit.'

I wasn't about to let Grandma force me to ruin her outing by telling her what I had seen. So I opened the box lunch, spread a napkin on her lap, and there I set her sandwich, sliced cucumbers and almond cookie. She lifted half of the sandwich.

'What is this? Smells like devilled ham.'

'It is devilled ham.'

'Starving.'

Must have been: she fucking gobbled it.

'I see you had another DUI.' You didn't see that, you heard it, and I could reliably assume that Mrs Devlin made sure of it.

'Yes, Grandma, drunk at the wheel.' Of course I was making light of this but secretly I thanked God it had stayed out of the papers. When you work with young children, it takes very little to tip parents into paranoia – they are already racked with guilt over dropping their darlings off with strangers in a setting where the little tykes could easily get shot or groped.

In families like mine, grandmothers loom large as yetis. I always thought having Grandma had been a blessing for me, but still I have often wondered if it wasn't her vigour that had made my father into such a depressed boob. He was a case of arrested development who never made a dime, but Grandma supported him in fine enough style for around here and at the far end of her apron strings. He was devoted to his aquarelles – his word. The basement was full of them. His little house has remained empty except for the flowers, bunnies, puppies and sunsets on every wall. Grandma says it's without a doubt a meth lab.

Perhaps I felt some of his oppression as Grandma sat bolt upright holding the other half of the sandwich ('I trust you washed up before handling my food.') and inhaling the mighty cottonwoods, the watercress in the tiny spring seeping into the broad, green and sparkling river. I thought about the drowned bridegroom sailing by, his arms fluttering like a bat. It was Grandma who'd taught me that every river has its own smell and that ours are fragrant while others stink to high heaven, catch fire or plunge into desert holes never to be seen again.

I think that at bottom some of these reflections must have been prompted by the mention of my latest DUI, which was a frightful memory. I knew it wasn't funny. I had left the Mad Hatter at closing, perfectly well aware that I was drunk. That was why I went there, after all. From the window at the back of the bar, as the staff cleaned up, I watched the squad car circle the block until I had determined the coast was clear. I ran through the cold night air to my car and headed up the valley. I hadn't gone far when I saw the whirling red light in my rear-view mirror, and there's where I made a bad decision. I pulled over and bolted out of the car headed into a pasture, tearing my shirt and pants on a barbed-wire fence. I didn't stop running until I fell into some kind of crack in the ground and broke my arm. That light in my rear-view turned out to be an ambulance headed further up the valley. I crawled out of the crack and got back into the car heading for the emergency room back in town. Drunk and driving with one hand I soon attracted an actual policeman and hence the DUI, the cast on my arm and this latest annoyance from Grandma, who may in fact be the source of my problems. I knew that thought was a tough sell which defied common sense but it was gathering plausibility for me.

I looked across the river at the row of houses above the line of car bodies. I heard a lawnmower over the whisper of river. A tennis ball came sailing over the bank, a black dog watching as it disappeared into the river.

Grandma said, 'When you were a little boy, I thought you would be president of the United States.' I got that odd shrivelling feeling I used to get when my parents couldn't handle me and she would have to come to our house. I decided to give her the silent treatment. She didn't notice. I watched as she took in all she could smell and hear with the same upright posture and air of satisfaction. I unexpectedly decided that I was entitled to a little liquid cheer and began tiptoeing in the direction of my car a good distance away – wasted tiptoeing, I might add, as Grandmother said, 'Bye-bye.'

I have no idea why starting the car and putting it in gear gave me such a gust of exhilaration that the quick stop for a couple of stiff ones seemed almost redundant. But that's what happened and I felt all the better for it as I walked into the sheriff's office just as Deputy Crane was leaving. I caught his sleeve and asked about the corpse. I could tell by his expression that he could smell the adult beverage on my breath. 'They pulled it out of the water at the Reed Point Bridge. I'm headed there now.'

'Oh, let me ride along.'

'What's the matter with you?'

Deputy Crane would have to get up earlier in the morning if he wanted to be rid of me. By the time he pulled out of town, I was hot on his trail. The interstate followed the river and we sped along doing seventy-five, the river intermittently visible on my left. Thus far the bridegroom had outrun us.

Pulling off the interstate and down into a riverside trailer park, I was convinced that euphoria was the rarest of all prizes, and being as good as anyone at cherishing mine, I started to fear that seeing the corpse up close might be a buzz-kill. A small crowd had formed at the riverbank and the squad car was parked close by. I pulled up next to the deputy who got out and, spotting me, said, 'Jesus Christ.' The small crowd parted at the sight of the uniform and I pushed through in its wake, was rudely asked to stop shoving. There within the circle of gawkers was the dead bridegroom. Either his wedding clothes were too small for him or he was seriously waterlogged. I don't know why they laid him out on a picnic table. The well-trimmed moustache seemed misplaced on the broad moon face whose wide-open eyes were giving me such a bad feeling. The gawkers would look at the face then at each other searching for some explanation. People with sideburns that long were inevitably from the wrong side of the tracks, where me and my family, excepting Grandma, had all lived. I couldn't say why I felt a corpse shouldn't have a moustache and long sideburns. It seemed about time to buck up with some more artificial elation. But first I thought it only right to inform this group that it was I who had first spotted our friend floating past. This fell on deaf ears. I looked around me with a bleak, ironic smile undaunted by their indignation.

Somebody at the Mad Hatter had told me there was going to be midget wrestling at the Waterhole. There was a van parked in front with the logo SUPPORT MIDGET VIOLENCE, but no midgets unless they were asleep inside. Two horses stood tied to the hitching rack in front by the trough, and beside them four pickup trucks with so much mud on the windshields that the drivers could only have seen through the wiper arcs. Between two of the trucks was a blood-red Porsche Carrera with New Mexico plates and a King Charles spaniel at the wheel. I was able to get what I wanted without giving the others the impression that I cared to mingle. The bartender was a compulsive counter wiper and when I got up the tip I left there disappeared. He pretended to find the bills under the rag as I departed, giving the entire crowd a laugh at my expense as I pushed through the doors. I thought of going back and raising hell but found the Porsche unlocked and released the spaniel instead. It was dark and all I could think of was one word: 'Grandma!' The dog headed off through the houses with their lighted windows as I was swept by uneasiness.

Something was making me drive this fast. I was trying my best to reckon where those little units of time had gone. Whatever trouble I was headed for it didn't feel like it was entirely my fault, just because someone decided to send a corpse through my day. If he'd lived on Grandma's side of town he would have enjoyed more options with no sideburns to maintain.

It was not easy to find our picnic site in the dark, and I wouldn't have been sure I'd found it if I hadn't spotted the remains of the box lunch. I ate the other devilled ham sandwich, the hard-boiled egg, the spicy pickle and the cookie, and staring at the large expanse of the river, breathing mostly with my abdominal muscles, I tried to collect my thoughts and ward off hysteria.

The chair was gone. So, she didn't jump in the river. Can't have more than one corpse a day. So somebody must have found Grandma and taken her home. This thought gave me an especially sharp pain as it suggested yet another person looking down on me, the oaf who left his blind grandmother on the riverbank.

I drove back across the Harlowton Bridge and through town heading for Snob Hollow, where Grandmother lived. My watch has a luminous dial, but I was afraid to look, fearing yet another buzz-kill. By the time I stopped in front of Grandma's I was having palpitations. I rifled the back seat in search of the minis sometimes scattered there but found only a mocking handful of empties. I stared through the windshield at the pair of juniper hedges leading to the door. My mind was so inflamed that when I got out of the car I thought I saw a face. I approached the front door and knocked, and then knocked again. Blood rushed to my head when I heard something within.

Mrs Devlin was fastening her terry-cloth wrapper at the neck. She was no girl herself, and those big teeth and accusing eyes only subtracted from any impression of innocence. She had led a blameless life and wouldn't say shit if she had a mouthful, but when backed by Grandma's authority she could be dangerous.

'You,' she said.

'Just checking in on Grandma.'

Then in the dark behind Mrs Devlin I heard Grandma ask, 'Is that him?'

'Yes it is, Meredith.'

'Mrs Devlin, kindly slap his face for me.' It sure stung.

I imagined saying, 'Try this one for size,' before throwing Mrs Devlin a roundhouse, but of course I just stood there as the door was slammed in my face. I headed back downtown, which in the dark looked abandoned, with so few lights that their silhouettes showed against the night sky, the blank face of the derelict mercantile, the bell cupola of the fire station with its mantle of cold stars. I returned to my room at the hotel, and the view of the mountains through the empty lobby, the old billiard table on which a century ago some surgeon treated the victim of a gunfight, the smells of mahogany and matted carpet, the dimmed lights gleaming off the souvenir cabinet. On my wave of booze and self-pity, one more nobody for the rest of the world to kick around. I pictured myself as the last survivor of my family, except for Grandma, who was left to contemplate what she had achieved over the generations. The thought lulled me into a nice sleep. I awakened to the sound of the breakfast dishes clattering in the restaurant, and for me a brand-new chance for success. As usual, whether I made the most of it or not, it would be fun just to see what happened, because, say what you will, I'm a glass-half-full kind of guy.

There wasn't time to eat before going to work, Mrs Hessler being a Nazi about punctuality. I was careful to avoid a long look at myself as I brushed my teeth and looked at my watch. I pulled on one of my work shirts, the one that says YOUR COMPANY NAME HERE at the top, YOUR LOGO HERE in the middle and ONE CHILD AT A TIME at the bottom. Mrs Hessler had gotten them in some close-out sale and expected to see me in them.

When I first went to work for Mrs Hessler, it was just after my casino years and, knowing about my résumé, she got me to teach her Texas Hold 'Em. She was pretty good but soon got overconfident and went off for a gambler's weekend to Vegas and lost her ass. Naturally she blamed me. That set the tone. I told her that in a world where sperm donors are expected to pay child support, anything could happen.

Hooray for me! I was actually early. I let myself into the playroom and realized I had never cleaned up on Friday. I had been in some haste to get to the Mad Hatter and so now, with so little strength, I would have to put everything in order before Hessler showed up and let me know by her silence how unhappy she was with me, her drone. I once told her I'd read that some archbishop staying at a five-star hotel in the Seychelles got his ass scorched on a rogue bidet. She didn't even crack a smile. Chutes and Ladders was all over the floor and I got dizzy picking up all the pieces. Moronic instruments for tiny mites – drums, tambourines, ocarinas – all would have to go on the 'music' shelf. The God Made Me Special poster had broken free of its thumbtacks.

I didn't remember so much chaos on Friday – motivational ribbons and certificates, birthday crowns, star badges, alphabet stickers all over the room – but then my mind had been elsewhere.

Frau Hessler closed the door sharply behind her to announce her arrival, made the rounds of the refrigerator, counted out the snacks in a loud voice, put the removable mopheads back in the closet, gave her own YOUR COMPANY HERE shirt a good stretch and greeted the first mother at the door. It was on. They came in a wave of noise as Hessler and I checked each other's faces for the required cheer. I had mine on good but felt like my teeth were drying out. Two mothers asked for the containers of their breast milk to be labelled and were quite abrupt telling me that Post-its would fall off in the fridge. The room was full of children, nearly babies, little boys and girls thematically dressed according to the expectations of their parents, little princesses and tiny cowboys, some still in pyjamas. Hessler always seemed to know exactly what to do and began creating order. I dove into the sock-puppet bins, trying to find one that felt right, pawing through the Bible-themed puppets, the monster puppets, the animal puppets. I was fixated on getting one I was comfortable with, since I'd ended up with St John the Baptist the previous week and Hessler rebuked me for failing to come up with relevant Bible quotes. Realizing I was running out of time by Hessler standards, I just snatched one randomly and found myself wearing an African American fireman hat and wiggling the stick that operated the hand holding the hose, all for the sake of a surly four-year-old named Roger. Roger was not amused and after a long silence called me 'Poopoo Head'. I offered up some goofy laughter, and Roger repeated the remark. 'In ten years, Roger,' I muttered, 'you'll be sniffing airplane glue from a sandwich bag.' I dropped the fireman on the bench and moved on to nicer children. I made it until Time Out, when I left the playhouse for a cigarette. A cold wind stirred the last leaves on the old burr oaks at the corner. Up on the hill, where Grandma's house stood, the sun was already shining. Mrs Devlin would be setting out her mid-morning tea and Grandma was sure to feel that things were in perfect order. ■

KRAPP HOUR

Anne Carson

Cast: KRAPP, *host*
      guests, various

Set: a TV talk show, minimal lighting, blackouts where marked. Kitchen chair for KRAPP, *couch for guests. Couch is not big enough for all guests, they gradually pile up. Guests are introduced by* KRAPP *briefly hoisting a placard from a pile under his chair.*

[enter KRAPP, K, to brief theme music]

K: not much you have to know about me, I need very little space and I like very little attention. Funny to end up here you may think, in this line of work, did I back into it, well more or less, I guess I did, yes and no, never mind, more important is other people do (need space, like attention), they come here, their eyes are bright, I love the brightness of their eyes, it is *ever* a surprise to me. If I had a family (I don't have a family) I cannot imagine they would look at me with such bright eyes. Admittedly there was a time I thought I would grow and flourish here, become happy and interesting and modern, well my old dad put paid to that notion the one time he came to the show – 'unchanged for the worse' he said and I believe I have adhered to that standard ever since.

[K holds up placard JACK KEROUAC AND HIS MOTHER GABRIELLE
(GABE), enter GK and JK]

GK: we're going to Radio City after this

JK: it's her birthday

GK: I'll be sixty-four where does the time go

K: where indeed

GK: I wasn't always this fat when I stopped wearing a girdle I
went all over the place

JK: say something in French Ma

GK: *qu'est-ce que tu veux savoir*

JK: you tutoyed him Ma, hear that she tutoyed you

K: so she did

GK: it's like that afternoon the Filipino butler kept giving me drinks

K: you've a butler

GK: no Barney Rosset's butler we went for dinner

JK: had a big screaming dinner all talking French Gallimard
was there *you're speaking pure eighteenth-century Norman
dialect* he said to me

GK: I played the piano then I went downstairs started kidding
the little butler I was having a ball

JK: later we hit the bars did Fifth Avenue supposed to have an
interview with *Holiday* magazine never made it

GK: Florida when we lived there he didn't drink at all but over
here oh my

JK: I can take it you know Li Po drank all those guys drank
dharma bums roaming China

K: Buddhists I suppose

GK: think I'd like a sandwich

[GK wanders off]

JK: whole thing's a sad mess

K: drinking you mean

JK: shallow journalism I mean, Cassady Ginsberg Burroughs
        with us you're talking the greatest American writers since
        the Transcendentalists and your name will go down with us
        or up with us, your name will go up

K: so I hope

JK: what we mean by shallow journalism is simply the failure to
        give complete tragic detail to your facts

K: the tragic detail I think I can capture

JK: I bet you're sincere I bet you're stringent but I don't know

[GK wanders back in]

GK: this is a way better interview than the one you did with Neal
        remember, what a waste of electricity taping all those *oh*s and *um*s

K: you mean Cassady

JK: Neal Cassady henchman Cassady Okie Dostoevsky
        Cassady I got the flash from his style

K: his books

JK: Cassady wrote no books Cassady wrote a forty-thousand-
        word letter to me in 1945 greatest piece of writing I ever
        saw spontaneous not crafty

K: where is it

JK: Ginsberg lent this ecstatic golden document to a guy on a
        houseboat in Sausalito who lost it

K: overboard

JK: I presume

GK: that Allen Ginsberg something about the man I couldn't stand

JK: she liked Cassady

GK: Neal was all right loved the horses that's why he was nervous

K: what is spontaneous writing

JK: *do not store up in your mind what you might say it is the Holy
        Ghost speaks through you* first time you've met the Holy
        Ghost I bet

K: almost, what does the Ghost say

JK: says I'm a messenger

[GK dozes off]

K: what is your message

JK: heaven is waiting for us, God is alone

K: you're a religious man

JK: religion darling is your own breaking heart

K: have you any bananas

JK: no but we could make a whiskey run

K: where to

JK: Elks Bar a few streets down, I'll go on with my story my story is endless you don't want to lose out on that, I lost out on things for instance 'Beat Generation' MGM's making a movie with that title but it's my title! we're going to sue, I was in church in 1945 kneeling all alone in the great silence and I realized beat means beatitude

K: in the sense beatific

JK: you see it doesn't apply to anyone else you see that

K: I have known such silence

JK: we get along all right don't we Krapp

K: get along we do

JK: go by the same rules, know what's my first rule

K: what

JK: Nothing Ever Happened so don't worry

K: know what's mine

JK: what

K: don't get drunk in your own house

JK: so let's go out

K: small point, I've got to stay and finish the Hour

JK: freedom is *out there* Banana Man

K: perhaps you'd bring me back one

JK: one freedom

K:	one banana
JK:	sure
K:	thanks
JK:	see you

[blackout, exit JACK KEROUAC]

[lights up and brief theme music, K holds up placard THOREAU'S AUNT MARIA, enter AM]

AM:	well we have to start somewhere
K:	it always feels like breaking into a locked room
AM:	shall we talk about me or Henry D
K:	as you prefer
AM:	I'm a shy person
K:	me too
AM:	let's not stare at each other

[AM gets up, lies down lengthwise on couch facing away from K, feet over GK who is still dozing]

AM:	I feel smarter this way
K:	I feel more polite
AM:	'there are no bad manners in the unconscious'
K:	who said that
AM:	my shrink
K:	you had shrinks in your day
AM:	you're kidding, yes electric shock therapy too of which let me tell you the worst part is the sound
K:	what sound
AM:	a tiny splash
K:	God save us
AM:	I no longer harbour that hope
K:	tell me what you hear now

AM: [puts hand over ears briefly] lamentation

K: ah

AM: very faint and far away

K: has your memory been affected

AM: I don't know let's test it, you heard the story of the gardener from Cincinnati

K: no

AM: a gardener runs up to his princess one day crying *Princess I've just met Death in the garden and he made a threatening gesture please lend me a horse to go over home* of course she lends him a horse

K: to go over home

AM: exactly, so later that day she meets Death in the garden

K: the princess

AM: yes

GK: [waking] they have a Princess of Cincinnati

AM: no the *princess* isn't in Cincinnati

K: oh

AM: and why are you asking that now

GK: I just woke up

K: let's talk about Henry D defaulting on his taxes

AM: advance in the direction of your dream he would say

K: he advanced to jail

AM: just one night

K: you paid the taxes

AM: yes

K: lot of money

AM: cost is relative

K: relative to what

AM: relative to the amount of life exchanged for it

K: did you pay his tuition at Harvard too

AM: check your facts young man, there was no question of arrears of tuition what Henry David refused to pay at Harvard was the five-dollar charge for a diploma

K: ah

AM: let a sheep keep its skin he said

K: do you ever get really tired of aphorisms

AM: yes

K: and then what

AM: and then I keep my peace

K: ah

AM: so the princess meets Death in the garden

K: how does she know it is Death

AM: I presume Death announced himself

K: really

AM: what do you mean *really*

K: I'd always imagined Death as wordless as having some sort
         of sound perhaps but wordless

AM: what sound

K: like poplars

GK: like popcorn

AM: well this story depends on Death being not wordless

K: I see

AM: we leave behind the logic of the everyday

K: agreed

AM: so the princess puts a question to Death in the garden

K: sorry, we have to take a short break here

AM: do I go or stay

K: as you wish

GK: can you move this knee

AM: I'll stay

[AM gets up, moves down couch, sits, blackout]

[lights up and brief theme music, K holds up placard MARTIN
HEIDEGGER, enter MH]

K: where were you in 1945

MH: —

K: Germany was at point zero

MH: —

K: perhaps it seemed the world would start over again

MH: —

K: you were beginning to think about Anaximander

MH: —

K: about justice and injustice paying the price to one another

MH: —

K: within the ordinance of time

MH: —

K: I was in Berlin the day the Russians entered for some
      reason I'm reminded of this now, they torched a
      whorehouse next to the zoo and you know the only image I
      cannot erase from my memory of war is tigers bears
      stags elephants roaming the Ku'damm some of them on fire

MH: —

K: look it's snowing

MH: [looks]

K: good thing we're sheltered here

MH: [brief sound]

K: I love that blue colour how it flows out and mingles with the
      evening

MH: —

K: as if a vein had been opened high up

MH: —

K: why don't you take the shorter way home

[exit MH]

K: I saw a singed baboon sitting on a park bench drinking a
      bottle of India ink

[snows briefly, blackout]

K: there was no shorter way home

[lights up and brief theme music, K holds up placard LA CHATTE
PROSECUTED FOR COLLABORATION WITH GERMANS PARIS 1945, enter LC]

K: you don't like questions
LC: no
K: how about subject headings
LC: go ahead
K: danger
LC: I found even as a child a thrill in danger
K: the Resistance
LC: I who had never read a spy story in my life
K: errors
LC: even small errors could be fatal
K: meals
LC: I ate meals before a mirror to feel less lonely
K: cat
LC: I was called *la chatte* perhaps for my fluid movements
K: Bleicher
LC: Bleicher offered me six thousand francs a month
K: pâté
LC: pâté with champagne was how Bleicher celebrated
       rounding up all the agents in my agenda
K: father
LC: father remained silent
K: mother
LC: mother screamed
K: villa
LC: coming and going from the villa I met gazes of hatred
K: sex
LC: sex was purely animal and it weighed against me at the trial
K: trial
LC: people who condemned me never knew me

K: facts

LC: in my deposition I have shortened them but retained all the actual facts

K: *épuration*

LC: 'cleansing' was for working-class women not Coco Chanel you notice

K: Coco

LC: got her name because she gave pretty good coke parties this was before the war, Nazis didn't care much for drugs

K: lawyers

LC: any fool can defend an innocent person takes talent to save a guilty one

K: last words

LC: I had some ready

K: last minute

LC: why de Gaulle came through who knows

K: guilt

LC: one is subtle or one isn't

[K holds up placard GHOST, enter G partly backwards]

K: can you turn around

G: no [turns partly]

K: is it your birthday

G: shreds

K: are you awake, asleep, do you sleep

G: how could I lose the address

K: you smell like stone

G: can you, what it how it how you learned to see it, as, something visible to or this object do they

K: first day of school you mean

G: they, shivering frail slow to a standstill around no you're no, more little dear no more closing the back of your *out you go* into

K: into what

G: I forget everyone forgets there's no way not to, hear that
       green snap this, what *out* is

K: how did you die

G: suicide

K: I'm sorry

G: I'm in the pines one day the sunrise falls out of the sky was
       that sin

K: oh no that wasn't sin

G: the rule I remember is no one can do both of both things
       but they must have been okay to do, it will be lingering in
       their mind the bruise of thinking how both, that both

K: you seem to be sinking or scattering or

G: I have no jokes I don't like jokes

K: I'm not joking

G: don't mean you

K: ah

G: night is hard on the lambs

K: have you no rest

G: you know it will end without anyone being free

K: what's that sound

G: everything in me falling

K: is there wisdom

G: A=A

K: what remains of all the misery

G: something mechanical

K: don't go

G: did you ever sing

[blackout which continues, snow continues]

[K and all guests in unison out of the dark whisper *yes*]

[blackout continues, snow continues, actors exit, light up on K's chair
with his shape left in snow] ∎

© DAVID BRANDON GEETING
Checkered Tile, 2013

THE MAST YEAR

Diane Cook

Jane stuffed as many of her belongings into her purse as she could. She'd just been called to her boss's office and she knew what that meant. Nothing good ever came from a visit to the boss's office. If she was about to be fired, she wanted her things with her.

But in her boss's office she didn't get fired. She got a promotion. With a raise – a good one. And a bigger desk. She unpacked her things and sank into her new, better chair. She'd often thought of quitting. The job had been stagnant. The commute was long. But this made it easy to stay. That day, she even enjoyed her drive home. The traffic seemed thinner and no one honked at her.

Then, that weekend, Greg returned from a business trip with a bulge in his pocket that turned out to be a ring box. Jane watched him slide the ring onto her finger. She thought about how, when Greg moved in, his things would mix with her things until they forgot who owned what. And there would be other perks of stability, like knowing what to expect and what was expected of her. She twirled the ring, enjoying its glimmer. It was as though the world had heard what she wanted and had finally decided to deliver.

This was how her year began. And shortly after, the first people arrived.

One morning, Jane found a man and woman sleeping in each other's arms near her roses. Jane figured they were homeless, though they didn't have that scruffy look. Perhaps they were drunk and had gotten lost. Their presence unnerved her, but she told herself they would leave in a day or so, and what was the harm?

The next day two tents stood under her willow. A few children ran around, and a man with a long beard moved landscaping stones into a circle.

During the night, Jane's sleep was disturbed by hammering. She woke to a crowd of men, women and children huddled under umbrellas, tents and tarps strung between the trees. There looked to be at least forty people. When Jane peered out the front door, they cheered.

She called her mother.

'Sounds like a mast year,' her mother said. Jane heard a game show in the background.

'You mean this is a thing?'

'Yes, it's a thing. It's a thing that happens to trees. But sometimes it happens to people too.'

Her mother explained that some years trees grew far more nuts than in ordinary years. A year of abundance was called a mast year. Somehow, as if the trees were calling to them, animals from all over sensed the tree's prodigious bounty and swarmed it. They gorged. 'I'll send you a book about it. It's short. More like a pamphlet.'

'But I'm not a tree.'

'You're like a tree. You drink water. You're tall. You're sweet.'

'Mom.'

'Jane. When people have mast years it's because they're having extra good fortune. Like you with your raise and engagement. Don't you think you're very fortunate right now?'

'Things are going well, but –'

'People want to join in your good fortune. So let them. You said to the world, "I've got something you want." You shook your limbs and said, "Come." So they came.'

'Sorry, Mom, but I didn't "shake my limbs". I didn't do anything.'

'Well, sorry, honey, but you did. They wouldn't be here otherwise.'

'Mom.' She wished she hadn't called.

'Jane, relax. You'll love it. You'll be surrounded by people who think you're wonderful. *Because you are.* They'll feel lucky. And you'll feel like a saint when it's over. It's only a year. What's one year?'

Jane wanted to tell Greg herself, but he'd already found out from work friends. He made a big show of ringing her bell and presenting her with flowers at the door even though he had a key and could have just come inside. Jane blushed and tried to usher him in, but he caught her around the waist and dipped her into a movie-style kiss. The crowd clapped their hands. Someone yelled, 'Woo!'

Greg called out, 'This woman loves *me*.' He puffed out his chest.

But once inside, Greg slumped. 'Why are you doing this?' he whined.

'It's just a thing that's happening,' she said.

'Well, make it stop.'

'I can't. I don't know how.'

'That's not what I heard.'

'Excuse me?'

'Aren't I paying enough attention to you?'

'Yes, you're fine. We're fine.'

'Then make them go away. They're going to think I don't do enough for you.'

'But you do.'

'Then why are they here?'

'I don't know.' She kissed his neck. 'Maybe I'm not doing enough for *you*.'

Jane tried to wake early so she could bring Greg breakfast in bed, but he was already in the kitchen when she came down. On the table was Greg's signature omelette, cut in two and plated, and mugs of coffee, hers fixed how she liked it.

'I also made a coffee cake, but it isn't ready yet,' he said. His brow seemed to frown.

'You make coffee cake?' She smelled vanilla and something bitter.

He glanced quickly out the window. 'I *always* make coffee cake,' he said, sounding hurt. The crowd looked hungry.

'Well, great,' she said, settling into a chair, 'I love coffee cake,' even though she thought it was just okay. 'Is it your signature coffee cake?' she asked, looking at her beige omelette.

'Why, yes. It is.' He laughed with relief, glancing out the window again. 'You're lucky. I'm a man with a signature everything.' His half of the omelette was gone, and he stood to go. He kissed her roughly, as though marking his territory. But then his kiss turned tender, and she blushed. The faces in the window were smeared with achy smiles.

'Be a doll and take that out of the oven in five,' Greg said, took two twenties from her wallet, and left.

She dumped the rest of her omelette into the trash. It was nice that he had signature things, but really *signature* just meant *one*, and his signature omelette wasn't very good. She tasted a corner of the coffee cake. It was salty. Jane cut it into pieces and arranged them on a platter. She would tell him she couldn't stop eating it.

As she pulled out of the garage, people gathered to touch her car. She triggered the door locks. Their clothing wiped the windows, metal buttons pinged the car like rain. Their faces showed deep concentration, as if they were placing a smell that had once been familiar. They held small trinkets in their hands, wood and stone talismans, stacked brownies tied with ribbons. They offered these to her.

'No,' she said from behind the glass. 'You keep those. I don't need them. Don't *you* need them?' The brownies looked good. Her mouth watered. But no, this was what it was all about. They were in need and she could give, and then they would leave, right? She inched the window down enough to slip them the coffee cake. Someone in a wool hunter's coat took it. 'Sorry, it's not very good,' she explained through the crack. 'I didn't make it. I will next time. I promise.'

They sniffed the cake and put crumbs to their tongues, tentative, she assumed, because she had claimed not to like it. She knocked on the window.

'Go ahead. It's good, it's fine,' she urged. They began to stuff chunks into their mouths. Their faces gave away that, truly, it wasn't good at all. She thought they might spit it out and leave, decide that if her first offering was crappy coffee cake, it wasn't worth the hassle. But they continued to eat it.

The news crews came. She saw her house on television. She saw herself, pre-taped, standing at her kitchen window, lit bright against the darkening evening, washing dishes, her hair static on one side and matted on the other. On-screen, she was wearing Greg's college track T-shirt, and she remembered it as the day they'd both called in sick just for fun.

She unconsciously smoothed down her hair.

After the news broadcast, people bloomed like mould across her yard, over where she'd planned to put a pool, threading through the forest border of the property. People climbed trees and built houses in them. She watched whole families disappear into the branches in the evening, then climb down each morning to pick through her garbage.

When the lawn and trees filled, people burrowed underground. They fought each other for shelter. Sometimes when people emerged from their burrows, others would be waiting to bash their heads, drag their limp bodies from the holes and then scurry in themselves. The victims would eventually come to and crawl away, embarrassed that even here their luck had run out. Wires fanned out from Jane's hacked electric and cable up into the trees and down all the holes, like streams off a mountain.

Jane had to bake for hours each morning. She bagged lunches for those who worked, passed out milk money to children lined up for the caravan of rerouted school buses, held babies so their mothers could get a shower in at the portable facilities Jane had rented. The people lined up before her, and Jane caressed each of their cheeks to give them strength for the day ahead. Then she drove to work. She was disappointed when her bosses suggested she begin working from home – productivity was down due to everyone wanting to stand around her. She liked work. Even more, she liked going to work and leaving her house behind.

'There were twelve birthdays that needed cakes today. And somehow they've got me tutoring all the fourth-graders. Can this not take too long?'

'Don't you think this is fun?' Greg said, smiling with all his teeth. '*I* think it's fun.'

'No, you don't.' Jane wouldn't use the word *fun*. She didn't think it was anything but exhausting to feel responsible for so many people.

Usually they peeled their clothes off in bed according to which body part they were trying to locate. But now Greg undressed slowly in front of the window. 'Come over here. I'd like to make you come over here.' Lately, he'd made a show of really enjoying it.

'No. The bed is a fine place for that.'

They fought over lights on or lights off and she won, but even in the dark she could tell when he peered out the window and flexed.

'It's so much better now,' he insisted loudly, rolling her into a different position. 'Don't you agree? I think I'm a better lover now. Don't you think I've become a better lover?'

'You're the same,' she said. She hadn't meant to sound unencouraging. He was going through a sensitive time. She tried to apologize by moaning loudly.

He lapped at her closest body part – her elbow – making a face like he was in a strange country, eating gross food his host family presented him. An *I love it* behind a false grin. She didn't like it either.

She situated herself on top of him and tried to pull a blanket over her shoulders, but Greg tore it off. She placed his hands over her breasts so anyone watching couldn't see them bounce. 'Nothing is different,' she whispered. 'And that's good.'

'Oh no,' he said. Then again, 'No,' and she thought he disagreed. Then he said, 'Yes,' like he'd reconsidered. And then again, 'Yes.' Then he came with theatrical force, almost bucking her off him. 'Wasn't that incredible?' he panted. 'Wasn't it incredible for you?' He acted more in love with her than ever, and so it felt like much less.

'It was great.'

'Let's go again. I'll do better.'

But Jane climbed off.

Greg's face drooped. 'Please,' he whimpered and gripped her.

Jane sensed the stillness of all the people outside, listening to them. The crickets were silent, as though listening too.

Her mother sent a thin, dog-eared paperback called *My Mast Year*. It had large print and clearly was self-published. On the cover, the author, Penny Smith, contemplated something soft in the distance.

Inside were gauzy photos of Penny baking pies, Penny reading to children by her fireplace, Penny cooking a shiny goose for what looked like thousands of people crowding her ornate dining room. They gazed at her with an aggressive love.

Jane had been generous, but she hadn't been gracious. She should think of this as an extended dinner party where everyone drinks too much and has to stay over. They should be comfortable and glad to be there. And in the sobering daylight, they would feel rested and satiated enough to leave.

She went to her front door, unlocked it, threw it open and went to bed.

At first, they were skittish; they hid as though they didn't believe her invitation had been genuine. But she'd catch clues that they'd been there during the night. Dirty mugs in the sink. New shows recorded on the DVR.

When Jane entered a room, a sense of movement lingered in the air. As if a minute before the room had been filled with people who'd hidden at the sound of her. She felt on the verge of a surprise party every time she flipped on the lights.

At night, she yawned loudly and said, 'I'm going to bed,' into the seemingly empty rooms. The house creaked to life once her light went out.

One morning, she came downstairs to a few people sitting around her kitchen table, digging into a pie she'd made the day before. They tensed, but they didn't run. They lifted their forks to her and one of them said, 'Good pie.'

Jane nodded. 'Thank you.'

From then on, people occupied every room. Late into the evenings they huddled in earnest conversation along every wall, lounged on furniture and on the floor, slept under and on the dining-room table. Their laughter drowned out her music, the radio news she liked to listen to. She believed they must be getting what they needed, and that she had helped them get it. But her house was now very crowded. The dishes were always dirty. There was never a chair to sit on. The shower drains were clogged with hair. She couldn't do any house-cleaning without being jostled. And no one helped. Each morning she had to shoo people out of the laundry room, where couples falling in love would go to be alone. She restocked toilet paper several times a day. She only found solace in her bedroom. She'd tacked a note on the door asking for privacy, which, thankfully, they respected.

On date night, Greg wrestled everyone out of the kitchen. 'Come back later,' he said. 'We're trying to have a romantic dinner because we're so in love.' The crowd regrouped in the kitchen doorway. Some of them threw pennies at him, which had become an insult in the house. Jane worried that people didn't like him. It made her self-conscious.

'You have to be nicer,' she warned.

'I'm nice.' He picked up a penny that had landed in his lap and chucked it back. The crowd booed.

Jane laid a seared steak in front of him, yawning.

'You should sleep,' he said.

She rolled her eyes. 'There's no time.'

They ate. When Greg had finished his steak, Jane passed him the rest of hers. 'Why don't you give that to them?' He was trying to be nicer.

She imagined them setting upon the meat like dogs, turning over lamps and tables, hurting each other. She would have to dress their wounds all evening. 'No, there's not enough.'

Just then a man sauntered into the kitchen. Like he owns the place, Jane thought, flushing with anger. She recognized him. He had a tent by her mailbox and went through her mail. She'd bought a shredder because of him. But she noticed the crowd of people in the doorway winking at her. A few gave her a thumbs-up sign, and she realized they liked this man.

'You gonna eat that?' the man drawled, pointing to the chunk of steak that sat between Jane and Greg.

'Who do you think you are?' Jane asked. She made her voice hostile, but really she wanted to know.

There was something rogue about him. Like he would be a bad addition to anyone's life. But his eyes were saggy and kind, like a dog's. He extended a hand. 'I'm West.'

'That's not your name,' she said, crossing her arms.

'No, but I wish it was.' He smiled then, and she could make out deep dimples hidden beneath his disorganized beard. The discovery made her blush.

Greg stood. 'Excuse me. This is a private dinner.'

West breathed deep. 'And what a delicious private dinner it is,' he said, and winked at Jane. 'Why don't you share?'

'I am sharing,' she said.

'Are you, though?'

What did he mean *share*? She felt like a victim of sharing. She'd tripled her grocery budget and had given in to the requests for sugar cereal. She'd instituted nightly storytelling around the bonfire for the children. As she spoke, those at her feet tied and untied her shoelaces or drew vines around her ankles. They stayed up past their bedtime because their parents took too many sips from the whiskey flasks they'd insisted she provide. The parents tottered around the yard flashing her tipsy grins. But other times she knew she'd displeased them. She'd taken on Greg's student loans in anticipation of their wedding. She'd heard grumbling that it meant less for everyone else. Was that what

West was saying? Was she expected to pay off everyone's loans?

She pulled the plate to her and methodically sectioned the meat. Greg said, 'Honey,' in protest, but West put up his hand and Greg quieted.

She chewed and swallowed each piece. She *mmm*ed like she loved every bite, though she thought she might be sick. West watched her mouth do this work, and then he smirked and winked again.

Later in bed, Greg pouted. 'Why did you eat the steak?'

The steak still felt lodged in her stomach. Like she'd eaten a golfball. 'You didn't want it.'

'But you *gave* it to me.' Greg rolled over and clicked the light off. 'You gave it to *me*.'

When Jane found herself in the same room as West, people winked and made kissing noises. Notes were passed to her at the kitchen table. *West likes you.*

'But I love Greg,' she would say.

They would shrug. 'But don't you like West?'

She did like West. She couldn't look at West without imagining his tongue on her skin. She wondered if he was a doting or selfish lover. She wanted him to be selfish. She thought from his smirk he might be, and she liked the idea of something that required no compromises, no special kindness, no giving. Just taking. She found the stuff of love hard to juggle with all the other stuff like cooking, cleaning, yard work. When Greg left for a week-long business trip, she felt relief for many reasons.

West became a fixture inside the house. He played music in the evenings, thumping out songs he'd written on the piano. Secretly, Jane liked to watch him play these songs, and at times she suspected that he played them for her. One must have been for her, because at the chorus West sang her name over and over again. The tune drifted into the kitchen, where she was sandwiched between two knitters, their needles and elbows jabbing her with each stitch. She could see West's back when he leaned in and out of the piano emotionally. The parlour was full of people, and they all laughed behind their hands and said,

'Aww,' like they'd just seen a baby. When West finished, everyone was quiet. From the ridge high above the house she heard the hollow echo of gunshots. Night hunting. Or someone else's mast year gone wrong.

Jane climbed the stairs to her bedroom, and they all watched her. She slid into bed and flicked off the light. A moment later West arrived and slid in beside her. She invited him to do what he wanted. She felt used and generous all at once. After, she asked if that was what he'd meant by sharing.

West moved in permanently. He brought nothing with him. As a first act, he transferred Greg's things to the front lawn where they were picked through by the crowd and eventually by a weepy Greg. West dealt with the mail, paid the bills, answered correspondence. Jane hadn't expected him to be helpful, but he was. He let Greg's loan payments default. She knew it was happening but pretended not to.

Inside the house, people patted her on the back.

'We never liked him,' they said of Greg. 'He was so needy. He tried too hard.'

Jane didn't bother to explain that he hadn't always been like that. He'd been fun; it had been nice, easy.

Her mother welcomed the news. She too had never liked him.

'If he was so awful, why did all these people come?' Jane asked. Now that her engagement was off, would they leave? That had been her hope.

'Oh honey, there's more to you than some boy and some job. Maybe there's something in you that's about to burst.'

Jane liked this idea.

Jane hadn't thought she wanted much from West. But he was steady and calm and she found herself relying on him more and more. As her feelings for him grew, so did the crowds. They doubled, then tripled. The old house shuddered under the weight. Parties went on all night. Sometimes into the mornings. The cushions of Jane's couch were deflated, all her curios had disappeared from her curio cabinet, all her books from her bookshelves. People drank and accused one another of slights. Fights broke out. People got injured. Ambulances came. The sirens screamed up and down her street, a seemingly endless loop of extreme alarm.

At night, Jane and West whispered under bed sheets so no one could hear.

'What made you come and live by my mailbox?' Jane asked him once.

'I just had a feeling I should.'

'I'm glad you did.' She felt him smile in the darkness.

West always fell asleep first, while Jane remained awake, holding him or holding his hand, listening to the night commotion in her house. All Jane wanted was to eat a nice, quiet dinner with West, to get to know him better without so many bodies pressing into them, living their love vicariously. But that possibility seemed farther away than ever.

On movie night, Jane and West couldn't find an empty spot on the couch. The floor was covered, head to toe. They stood in the corner and balanced their beers and popcorn. People grabbed fistfuls from their bowl until the popcorn was gone. They wiped their buttery hands on Jane's pants.

A large plaid-clad man was controlling the remote. A home-renovation show was on.

West tried pulling rank. 'It's movie night.'

The large man said, 'It's *Ace the Wrecker* marathon night.'

Others called out the news, trivia or crime shows they wanted to watch.

West contested, 'But I signed up for this time. It's movie night.'

Everyone turned to Jane for a final verdict. 'Leave me out of this,' she snapped.

The large man catcalled, 'You could use help around here. I can build an addition in exchange for a little –' He made a lewd gesture.

Jane dropped West's hand and pushed through the crowd toward her room. The people pushed back. She stepped over heads and the hands that reached for her, groped at her ankle, her knee. They tried to reach higher. They pulled at her sweater, clutched at her belt. Arms looped around her waist. Her hair was yanked. She scratched her way out.

When she slipped into bed, she found four children hiding under the comforter, a rumple she thought was just bunched sheets. The children clung to her and called her Mommy. She could not free herself, so she lay limp while they mewled. West arrived and peeled the children from her and scooted them out the door.

All night, the house stairs creaked; people thudded down hallways, in and out of rooms, slamming doors, laughing, yelling, fighting. Music blared, people fucked, moaned, glass broke. Jane shook. West held her and stroked her hair.

'Hang in there, kiddo,' he said. 'It's only July.'

She turned from him and wept.

Jane woke alone. She smelled bacon and knew West had cooked for her. He was always doing small, thoughtful things.

He sat at her kitchen table, but so did forty others. They left no place for her. People perched along the counters, their heels banging against her cupboards. All the burners burned, the microwave buzzed, the oven was on broil. Something even cooked over a fire in her fireplace.

West looked up at Jane from the newspaper, ratty and worn as if it had already been read a hundred times that morning. Two plates of breakfast sat in front of him. He had waited. Seeing her, he picked up a strip of bacon and held it under his nose like a moustache, even though he had a full beard. Desire thrummed in her, and she said, 'You're so cute,' but it was drowned out by all the morning noise. He smiled, but she knew he hadn't heard her.

From over by the toaster, Jane heard yelling. More voices joined. A scuffle erupted. Something about a piece of cinnamon toast. People surged rapidly to escape the fight and both of Jane's feet left the floor as she was pressed upward by the bodies around her. She screamed. The nearest people shrunk from her and she fell to her knees.

She had lost sight of West, but she heard him call out, his voice full of concern but far away. 'Are you okay?'

Jane couldn't speak. She punched her way through the crowd, wanting to harm, and once inside her bedroom, slid all the furniture in front of the door, even the wicker hamper which held only one sock. Someone had stolen all her dirty clothes.

By lunch, West was able to force himself into the bedroom. Jane sat stiffly in bed. He approached with caution, as if she was either delicate or dangerous. He tried to hold her.

'Don't touch me,' she said coldly.

His eyes widened. 'Why not?' He tried to hold her again.

'I don't want people touching me.'

'But it's me,' he said, his voice soft with confusion. 'I'm different.'

He was different. That was the problem. 'You need to go,' she said.

'But I can help. Let me help you.'

'Help? You can't help me. I don't even love you.'

'That's not true,' he said.

'Yes, it is,' she said, through tears now. 'Get out.'

'You do too love me. I can see it.' He tried to sound certain, but he shook his head, stunned.

'You're wrong. This whole world was wrong. I have nothing to give you. So leave.'

'Honey, you don't really believe that. That's not what you want.'

'You have no idea what I want.'

'So tell me.'

But she didn't know what to say. She felt a strong desire to be alone, but she didn't know how long that feeling would last. And she didn't equate that desire with knowing what she really wanted. She said nothing.

West smoothed her cheeks, but he failed to find her behind hardened eyes, and so he reluctantly packed a bag, a bag he hadn't arrived with, full of things that didn't belong to him, and left.

News spread through the house, out to the yards, up the trees and underground. Conversations died in the living room. People quickly got out of Jane's way when they saw her coming. For the first time in what felt like years, she went a full day without brushing shoulders with someone.

When the food ran out, she didn't buy more. People scrounged in the garbage, hunted for scraps in the yard. The hunger set in. Motley caravans began to leave, clanging down the streets at all hours. People insisted Jane buy supplies to make them snacks and bagged lunches for the road, pay their bus fare, drive them to the airport. 'You owe us,' they said, but she gave them nothing. They threw pennies at her, then collected what fell at her feet. They would need them.

'Mom, they're leaving.'

'What did you do?'

'I kicked West out.'

'Oh honey, why?'

'I don't know. They steal my stuff.'

'You have plenty of stuff.'

'It was too much. I couldn't take it.'

'How am I not surprised? You have no follow-through. You never have.'

'Mom.'

'Jane. What's one year? You were happy. They were happy.'

'I wasn't happy.'

'Well, is this what you wanted?' her mother said. 'Now who's happy?' ∎

MIRAGE

Claire Vaye Watkins

'There it is. Take it.' – William Mulholland

R ay had the blazing prophet eyes of John Muir and like John Muir war left him nerve-shaken and lean as a crow. He returned loaded with worry and, he said, the ocean saved him. The way he told it a city of a ship deposited him in the new riverless West at Long Beach. He was never so soothed as that first day in the white noise of the breakers, so instead of going home he filched a surfboard from someone's backyard and made his home in the curl. He had a mind to surf through all crises and shortages and conflicts past and present. He was surfing the day they pronounced the Colorado dead and he was surfing the first day it was dammed, a hundred years before. He surfed as the Los Angeles aqueducts went dry and he surfed as Mulholland inaugurated its first. He surfed while new aqueducts stretched to the watersheds of Idaho, Washington, Montana, as a concrete waterway crept up to Alaska, where the Mojave Desert licked the base of a glacier. He surfed as John Wesley Powell pointed his rafts down the Green River with the one arm the minie balls at Shiloh had left him. As the Central Valley went salt flat, as FarmCorps drilled daily three thousand feet into the unyielding earth, praying for aquifer but delivered nothing but hot brine.

Then, one day, Ray emerged from the thrashing oblivion of the Pacific at Point Dume and there was a chicken-thin, gappy-toothed girl there, crying off all her eye make-up.

Seawatery, gulping air and clutching his board to his side, Ray approached her. What was the first thing he said? Luz could not now remember, but it would have been sparkling. She did recall his hands, gone pink with cold, and his pale aqua prophet eyes, and herself saying in response, 'I haven't seen anyone surfing in years. I forgot about it.'

Ray's hope was naked when he asked, 'You surf?'

She smiled, thinly, and shook her head. 'Can't swim.'

'Serious? Where you from?'

'Here.'

'And you can't swim?'

'Never learned.'

They sat quiet for a time, side by side in the sand, hypnotized by the unquitting waves.

'Where are you from?' she said, wanting to hear this wildman's voice again.

'Indiana.'

'Hoosier.'

'That's right.' He smiled. He had an incredibly good-looking mouth.

'Why d'you come here?'

'I was in the military.'

'Were you deployed?'

He nodded.

'What did you do?'

He snapped a seaweed polyp between his fingers and smiled. 'You've heard that dissertation.'

He said his name and she said hers and then they sat quietly. At their backs, coral and shimmering in the sunslant, was a de-sal plant classified as defunct but which in truth had never been funct. They'd heard that dissertation too.

Luz asked, 'You going to evac there, Indiana?'

'Nah.'

'Where, then?'

'No where.'

'No where?'

'No where.'

He told Luz about the sea and his needing it, that California had restored him, that he would not abandon her, a sentiment shared by many in those early days of evacs. But Ray was the first person Luz believed. He said he felt even, for the first time. He had purpose here. Had she ever felt that way? She had not, but soon would.

'What are you going to do, then?' she asked.

'Some people I know have a place. Even if they didn't. Hoosiers aren't quitters. California people are quitters. No offence. It's just you've got restlessness in your blood.'

'I don't,' she said, but he went on.

'Your people came here looking for something better. Gold, fame, citrus. Mirage. They were feckless, yeah? Schemers. That's why no one wants them now. Mojavs.'

He was kidding, but still the word stung, here and where it hung on factories in Houston and Des Moines, handpainted on the gates of apartment complexes in Knoxville and Beaumont, in crooked plastic letters on the marquees of Indianapolis elementary schools: NO WORK FOR MOJAVS. DIRTY MOJAVS KEEP OUT. MOJAV THIEVES NOT WELCOME. A chant ringing out from the moist nation's playgrounds: *Watch the Mojavs dry to dust! Let them burn then sweep them up!*

Ray smiled and his sweet mouth soothed her. 'We're stick-it-out people,' he said, but what he really meant, she knew, was they could be Mojavs together.

'You look like I know you,' Ray said. Had he seen her before? Luz said maybe and sheepishly described the decaying billboard lording over Sunset Boulevard, a photo taken the year she turned twenty-four but was writing eighteen on all her forms, the year her agency relocated to Austin without her. Her in Italian bra and panties, eyes made up into beautiful bruises, crouched over a male model's ass like she was about to take a bite of it. One papery panel peeling off, so her bare legs looked shrunken, vestigial.

Ray said, 'No, somewhere else.' Then Luz kissed him.

After, there was more quiet between them.

Then Ray asked, 'What about you? You're going to evac?'

The Department of Interior took you by bus. She hated crowds, hated every human being except for this one. She suddenly and fiercely did not want to get on that bus tomorrow, as scheduled. Luz, frightening herself a little, said, 'I was.'

So Ray took her home, to Santa Monica, to the gutted apartment complex where his friends had set up camp, and which they would abandon for the starlet's canyon mansion when things with the friends went south. They had sex on Ray's bedroll in the laundry room. After, she said, 'I need you to promise me something. Promise me we won't talk about the drought any more.'

'Wouldn't dream of it,' he said.

Dusk was coming to the dry rills of Venice Beach. Luz followed Ray along the berm and into a man-high rusty corrugated drainage culvert, where the berry man was supposed to be. Inside, a stench met them, faecal and hot. Something scraped about back in the darkness, something else screeched. As the light at their backs wilted Luz put one hand to her mouth and groped for Ray with the other. This was, suddenly, not a good place to be a woman.

The starlet's sandals began to slice into her heels again and Luz stumbled. 'You okay?' Ray whispered. She nodded though she was dizzy and hot and there was a new pressure on the underside of her eyebones, and though Ray surely could not see her.

Soon Luz's pupils dilated wide enough to accept Ray's silhouette ahead of her, embarking on his errand. She clung to him with one hand and traced the other along the metal wall of the tunnel, flinching at rust splinters and steadying herself as she lurched over knee-high sediment dunes and dry knolls of sewage. She wanted to forge ahead, but did not know the way. The pair forked into a smaller culvert where Ray had to stoop. The sounds in the tunnel went human now, voices of people gathered to haggle and score ricocheted down the tube. *Fresh socks here, all cotton socks. Ovaltine, whole can, hep!* Luz and Ray continued and soon the culvert was clogged with the crowd's collective fetid lethargy. Wherever they walked, bodies and the outlines of bodies blocked their path. Ray lobbed the words *blueberries* and *Seattle* into the darkness and what came back was *Not me, hep. Deeper brother,* and then, *Um hm. Careful, he nasty.*

Finally Ray tossed *blueberries* and was met with *Here, son.* From the darkness materialized a shirtless daddy-o, bald head glistening, tiny mouth gnawing on a black plastic stir straw. Beside him stood an ashy-skinned brother with scarred-up hands and a backpack from which he retrieved a drained ration cola can.

The daddy-o held it aloft in the darkness. 'One-fifty.'

Ray took the can and examined it. He handed it to Luz. She shook it and a handful of berries padded inside the aluminum. The daddy-o said, 'Easy, darlin'.'

She put the can to her nose and smelled barely the dulcet tang of them.

'Give you seventy-five,' said Ray.

The daddy-o gestured reverently to the can. 'Son, these is some juicy-ass berries. Juicier than juicy pussy.' He winked at Luz. 'Can't give them up for less than a hundred.'

'Eighty then.'

'Eighty,' the daddy-o said to his partner. He sucked his teeth.

The partner said, 'Used to be a nigger could make a living in this city.'

'That's all I got,' said Ray, though it was not.

'All you got,' said the daddy-o. He reached out to retrieve the can from Luz. She handed it over. But instead of taking the can from her, he torqued his long-nailed index finger through the starlet's tennis bracelet, still strung like dewdrops around her bony wrist. Luz pinched her breath in her throat. The daddy-o said, 'I doubt that.'

'Hey guy,' said Ray, but Luz was saying, 'Take it,' her fingers panicking against the wretched little clasp.

The daddy-o flung Luz's own hand back at her. 'The fuck you think I am?' To Ray he said, 'One hundred.'

Ray gave him ten ten-dollar bills, took the can of berries and turned. Luz's sense of direction had left her. It was all she could do to follow Ray, who was dissolving into the darkness then rematerializing to tug her along.

'Christ,' he whispered, meaning *Christ, be more careful* and *Christ, I love you and you're all I have and therefore you have an obligation to take care of yourself.* Luz looked ahead, needing a glimpse of the daylight they'd left, but she saw only bodies, bodies. Someone trampled her heel and she stumbled. She needed to get away from these fucking people. Then, mercifully, Ray led her into a dark, clear space.

Her eyeballs registered the solid perimeter of people they'd broken through. Their mouths hung open dumbly, and they were staring at her. They were not staring at her. Luz followed their gaze and saw, beside her, an old woman sitting on a metal folding chair. She wore a dress that had been festooned mightily in its day but was now threadbare and freckled with cigarette burns. She wore watersocks, pair of obsolescence, and on each of her livery shoulders was a macaw, one red and one blue.

The circle of bodies pressed in closer. The red macaw pinched a nut or a stone in its beak, working at it with its horrid, digit-like black tongue. It twitched its head. It blinked its tiny malarial eye.

Suddenly Luz was breathing everyone else's foul, expelled air and Ray was somehow angry and gone and there was only so much air down here and everyone was sucking it up and where was he? Had he not heard of girls carried up out of the canal into one of the vacant houses whose dry private docks jutted overhead, homes once worth three and four and five million and which were now every one of them humid with human fluids? Had he not been with her the night she'd seen a woman stumble out of one of the houses, used and bewildered, make her way back down to the canal toward the music, only to be dragged back up again?

Luz stepped back from the birds and collided with a sickle-thin teenager. He wore a black T-shirt with some meanness written on the front and sagging holes where the sleeves should have been. Through these holes flashed his tattooed cage of a chest. There was a long tear up one leg of his jeans and along it dozens of safety pins arranged like staples in flesh. He held a rope and at the end of it was a short-haired, straw-coloured dog, wheezing. The boy laid his rough hand on the bare skin between Luz's shoulder blades. He rubbed.

'Easy, sweetheart,' he said and from his mouth escaped the scent of rot.

Something leaden and malignant seized Luz's heartmuscle. She wrenched away. 'I can't breathe,' she said, barely.

Ray turned to her.

'What?'

'I can't breathe.'

'What do you mean?'

'I'm dying.'

He put his hand on the back of her neck.

'I can't breathe,' she said. 'I fucking can't breathe.'

Ray didn't laugh at this, though it was laughable. Luz knew it was even now, except the knowledge was buried somewhere in her beneath bird tongue and daddy-o and sweetheart asphyxiation.

'You're okay,' he said. 'Listen.'

She gripped his T-shirt in her hands and pulled. 'I can't *breathe*, Ray.'

'You're all right,' he said. 'Tell me.'

One of the birds went *wrat wrat*, impossibly loud, and Luz flinched. *Wrat* again and she began to claw at Ray's midsection. People were looking at them now, laughing, and she had an idea to open up her boyfriend and crawl inside him.

Ray took Luz's two scrambling hands in one of his like a bouquet and looked her in the eyes. 'You're okay,' he said again. 'Tell me.'

'I'm okay,' she said, though she was also dying.

'Tell me again.'

She breathed. 'I'm okay.'

'We're walking,' said Ray, taking her by the shoulders.

They walked and breathed and walked and breathed and soon a dim disc floated ahead of them. Ray led her to it, miraculously, Luz saying, I'm okay, I'm okay, I'm okay, I'm okay.

Their blanket – a duvet meant for guests of the starlet – was still under the footbridge when they got back, another miracle amid the rampant pilfering. Ray sat Luz down. He passed her his ration jug. She refused it and he passed her hers.

He watched her as she drank.

'Thank you,' she said after some time.

'Do you want to go home?' he asked. He wanted to see the bonfire, she knew. 'It's fine if you do.'

What she wanted was an Ativan and a bottle of wine, but those days were over.

It was cooler in the canal and the air was freshish, or at least it moved. The long shadows of Venice stretched to shade them and the blanket had not been taken and there was Ray, trying. She told herself to allow these to bring her some comfort.

'No,' she said. 'Let's stay.' She sat on the blanket and breathed. Eventually, Ray asked whether she wanted to go back to the drum circle.

'Can we just sit here a while?' she said.

'Sure.'

'Sorry.'

'Don't be,' Ray said, which was what he always said. He motioned for her to lie back and rest her head in his lap. She did. She fell asleep and dreamt nothing.

She woke needing to pee. It was nearly dark but fires were glowing along the spine of the canal and the big bonfire was down the way, throbbing brightest of all. Ray had taken his shoes off and was lying on his back writing in his notebook. Luz lay still, studying him in the smoky light: his willowy hands, his steady chest, the tuft of black hair in the divot between his collarbones, barely visible above the neck of his T-shirt. His flat, slightly splayed feet. Everything about him suggested permanence. She rose and kissed him on the head. 'I have to pee.'

Ray set the notebook aside. 'It's okay,' she said, sober and wanting badly to be off his list. 'I'm okay.'

Luz made her way up the wall of the canal. The trench beyond was dark and balmy with stink but she was feeling much better. She straddled the trench, lifted her dress, urinated into the hole, shook her ass some, then stood. Yes, she was feeling better. The sun had gone down and the canal was cooling off, the nap had dissolved the throb in her head. She was okay. She would have some more water, eat something. There were blueberries in Ray's backpack and more mash in the growler. She was all right. They would go back down to the drum circle. They would dance. She would not ruin Ray's fun after all.

Descending the smooth dusty pitch of the canal she looked down at the bonfire and then beyond it, where someone had sent up a firework. She saw the little puff of smoke and heard its snap and exactly then – the instant the sound of the bottle rocket reached her, ever-searing the moment into her memory as a kind of explosion – something slammed into her knees, nearly toppling her. She looked down to see a trembling, tow-headed toddler wrapped around her legs.

Luz could not remember the last time she'd seen a little person. The child was maybe two years old, a girl, it seemed. She wore only a shoddy cloth diaper, its seat dark with soil. She looked up at Luz with eyes like grey-blue nickels, sunk into skeletal sockets. Her skin was translucently pale, larval, and Luz had the sense that if she checked the girl's belly she might discern the shadows of organs inside.

'Hi there,' Luz said.

The child only stared unblinkingly with her coin eyes.

'Are you lost?' asked Luz. 'Where's your mommy?' The girl's forehead bulged subtly above the brow and she pressed it now into Luz's crotch. She tried to pry the girl from her legs but the child clutched tighter and let loose a high, sorrowful moan.

'Shh,' she said. 'You're okay.' She patted her on the back. Without thinking Luz put her fingers in the child's white-blonde hair, tufted at her nape like meringue.

Soon, she managed to separate from the girl long enough to kneel. The girl squirmed to re-establish herself in Luz's lap, hinging her thin arms around Luz's neck. Luz held her, feeling the girl's torso struggling with sobs. Luz expected someone to come for the girl but no one did. No one was paying any attention to them.

Then, the girl stopped crying. She regarded Luz a moment, then reached one hand up and laid it plainly on Luz's face, partially covering her right eye. The small hand was moist with saliva, slick as a wet root.

'Where's your mommy and daddy?' Luz said again.

The girl ignored the question if she understood it. She rotated her hand so it lay across Luz's brow. The child pinched her mouth in concentration. She pressed, then positioned her other hand at Luz's jaw and pressed again. Luz felt uncannily at ease, as though the raindance had slipped away and left the two of them alone in the smoky twilight, the campfires pulsing like lures in the distance. Luz smiled, and the child smiled too, and when she did Luz felt an unbearable welling of affection, both for the girl and from her. She had not been needed in a very long time.

With her hands still at Luz's face the girl said, 'Piz kin tim eekret?'

'Tim eekret?' Luz tried.

The child squenched her face in frustration. 'Piz can I tell you a secret?' she repeated.

'Oh,' said Luz. 'Okay.'

The girl stretched to Luz's ear and began to speak. Luz strained and only after a moment realized the child was not saying anything, only replicating the feathery sounds of whispers: *spuh, spuh, spuh, spuhst.*

When she finished the girl leaned back and said gravely, 'Don't tell, okay?'

'Okay.'

'Don't tell *anyone*.'

'I won't.'

A figure strode through the dusk and toward them. It was Ray, looking purely mystified at Luz where she knelt on the ground whispering with a child. A *child*, for Christ's sake. 'What's going on?' he asked.

'She's lost,' said Luz.

'Did you ask around?'

'It just happened.'

Another figure drew near them. As he came closer Luz recognized the teenager who had touched her in the sewer: his caved torso, the track of safety pins along his torn jeans. Several heavy chains drooped between his back pocket and a belt loop, swaying as he approached. The white font on his black shirt read I KNEW I WAS A NUT WHEN THE SQUIRRELS STARTED STARING. His eyes were on the girl.

'Get the hell over here,' the Nut said to the child. He pointed down the berm, and Luz became aware of a scattering of rangy, dull-eyed young men camped out on the canal bottom, shirtless and unwashed. They cradled mash growlers and other incovert alcohols, one gripped a filthy glass water bong. The straw-coloured dog scavenged among them, the rope still tied around its neck but trailing now behind him. Among the men were two girls, teenagers. The first straddled a man whose age was easily a multiple of her own. His one hand pinched a filterless cigarette while the other grazed beneath the girl's tank top. His thick arm pulled her top up and the knuckles of the girl's spine rose as she bent to take the man's tongue into her mouth. The second girl was heavy, with rounded shoulders, large breasts drooping into a bikini top and a doughy midsection spilling from tight jean shorts. She watched Luz through hair cespitose and greenish from ink dye, not with anger or concern, not with anything except perhaps a dumbness that left her mouth slightly open. Under this dead gaze Luz realized she was still cradling the child.

Luz pointed to the second teenager. 'Is that your mommy?'

The child shook her head. *No.*

The Nut said, 'Her mommy's not here.' The tattoo on his bicep was a smeary green cross whose blurred lines and imperfect proportions summoned rumours Luz had heard about Mojavs inking each other with sewing needles and Bic pens. The cross came closer now as the Nut bent to take the child by the arm. The baby – as Luz had come to think of her, though she was not a baby – scrambled into Luz's lap and flung her arms around Luz's neck. Luz looked up at the Nut. She did not want him to take the baby, but he would, of course.

Ray laid his hand on Luz's shoulder, protecting her from the Nut or from herself. Luz rose, forcing the child to slide from her lap. 'Time to go,' Luz told her.

'No, no, no!' the girl cried.

The Nut took the child's arm roughly and the girl screamed, 'Okay!' She wrenched her tiny arm from him. 'But please can I tell her a secret?'

The Nut rolled his eyes and nodded and Luz bent down again, letting the child up to her ear. Ray looked on. Again the girl made whispering sounds but said no actual words. When she was finished she looked at Luz and said, 'Tell everyone, okay?'

Luz said, softly, 'Okay, I'll tell everyone.'

'And come back to me.'

Luz glanced up at Ray. 'I can't come back to you,' she said to the baby. 'I have to *go.*'

'Okay, but please can I tell you a secret?'

The Nut exhaled loudly but Luz leaned down to the girl again. The child made no breathy sounds this time, but spoke clearly: 'Please may I have a glass of water?'

Luz stood, and in the tone adults use to speak through children she said, 'I'm sure your friends can get you a glass of water.'

The Nut once again took the girl by the arm. As he left he told Luz plainly, 'We don't have any water.'

Luz watched him pull the baby back to the group, where he sat her down between the doughy teenage girl and the man with the bong. He said something sharp to the child, but Luz could not tell what.

Ray took Luz's hand. 'Let's go,' he said, though his face looked as sick as hers must have. They walked toward their blanket. Luz looked back but already the girl was out of sight, blocked by a stand of partakers. They walked on.

It was Ray who spoke first. 'That didn't seem right.'

Luz stopped. 'Let's go back,' she said.

'And do what?'

'Watch her. Make sure she's okay.'

'Why?'

'What if those weren't her people?'

'What do you mean?'

She took a short breath, knowing how the next part would sound. 'I have a feeling.'

Ray frowned and swept a strand of hair from her eyes. 'Sweetheart –'

'I'm not drunk any more,' she said, though she was not sure if that was true.

'I didn't say you were.'

Luz's voice changed. It begged. 'Let's go back, just to see if everything looks okay.' Ray ran his hand up and down her bare arm, as if she were cold. She wasn't cold but she was trembling. 'Please,' she said.

Ray looked back toward where they had left the girl. 'All right.'

They walked a wide loop into and out of the canal and circled back on the other side of the footbridge. They stopped where they could spy down on the girl. The canal had gone from gleaming grey and bleach white to fireglow and a misty blue-black. They turned to face each other, pretending to talk the happy talk of young people in love.

Luz stood with her back to the canal with Ray looking over her shoulder. 'Do you see them?' she whispered.

Ray nodded. 'There.'

'What are they doing?'

'The same thing. Sitting.'

'Do you see her?'

'No.'

Luz knew instantly that something unspeakable had happened to the girl, and that it was her fault. She resisted the rising urge to turn.

Ray's eyes raked the chaos of the canal beyond. 'Wait,' he said. 'There she is.'

'What's she doing?'

'She's playing. Running around.'

Luz could not stop herself from turning now. She spotted the girl stepping softly in the hot silt, alone. Beyond the child, the Nut and the girl who was not her mother and all the rest were back in their circle, taking rips from the bong, playing roughly with the dog. The thin girl was kissing a different man.

Luz and Ray watched the child – this coin-eyed, translucent-skinned child. She approached a young woman with a ragged mohawk, who sat cross-legged on the concrete slope. The woman wore a crinkly purple skirt and a canvas backpack. She was topless and her breasts had been painted as two drooping purple daisies, her nipples the polleny yellow cores. The child hopped forward now and waved her hand emphatically in the young woman's face.

'See,' said Ray. 'She does that. Goes up to people.'

The topless woman said something and the girl solemnly rose up to touch the woman's mohawk. She pancaked the inky flattened wall of hair between her two hands. The woman laughed, perhaps uneasily. Ray put his hand between Luz's shoulder blades, where the Nut had first touched her. 'She's just a weird kid.'

The child brought her hands to the woman's face and rubbed it all over, as she had done to Luz, and Luz was betrayed, preposterously. 'You're right,' she said.

Ray stepped toward the bonfire, urging Luz in that direction with his large hand. But after a few yards Luz shook him off. 'You saw the way she grabbed me,' she said. 'She was afraid of him.'

'You don't know that.'

'I have a feeling. I don't want to ignore it.'

'What do you want to do?' he asked, kindly. He was handling her.

He thought her drunk and sliding toward hysteria, though he knew better than to put it that way. They'd been here before.

'Can we move our stuff over here?' Luz asked.

'What?'

'They don't have *water*, Ray? What does that *mean*?'

'I'd just like to know what you hope to gain here. Your goal.'

'They're taking her rations, probably.'

Ray sighed. 'If it will make you feel better.'

They fetched their things and rearranged them on the other side of the footbridge, where they could see the girl and her people. Luz could not take her eyes from the child as she flitted through the raindance, darting around fires and garbage heaps, collecting sticks and stalks of shimmering trash into a bushel in her hand. She was a weird kid. She just went up to people. Yes, but it was also true that some evil was going down here and Luz knew she was the only one who could see it. For the first time in her life, she was absolutely essential, activated and very much alive.

'I am acutely engorged with purpose,' she whispered. Ray said to have some more water, but she would be on no one's list ever again.

Luz eavesdropped on the group shamelessly and caught some of their words – *ream, whore, fuck rag, come dumpster* – words Luz herself had used, of course, and whose explicitness had always delighted her, but which seemed now repugnant.

'Did you hear that?' Luz would ask. But Ray was making a show of eating almonds. He was, he said, through spying on people. Luz was not through. Not hardly. She was spellbound by the group's filth and their tremendous youth and their drug-depleted gazes – indeed the more she watched them the more they embodied stories she'd heard of vile things happening in the Valley. Even the weeds shocked through the cracks in the concrete nearest them were deader than the others.

The child spotted Luz once more, smiled a kinked smile and ran to her. It wasn't until Luz saw this all-out tottering run that she recognized how she ached to hold the girl again. The baby bowled into Luz, toppling happily into her lap.

'Hi,' said Luz.

The girl said nothing, only stared up at Luz. With dusk her chameleon eyes had gone a milky heather, her hair silver. She smelled strongly of urine.

'Are you thirsty?' asked Luz.

The child opened and closed her mouth like a carp.

'Want some water?' Luz tried, holding up her ration jug for the girl.

The child squealed and lunged for the jug. Luz unscrewed the cap and the baby drank heartily and with some difficulty, spilling down her bare chest and letting out big wet gasps between gulps. Ray watched fondly, despite himself. Luz fetched the blueberries from the backpack.

'You hungry?' she said. Ray glanced over to the Nut and the others. Luz wilted, expecting the Nut to retrieve the girl again. Instead, he waved. Not a friendly wave, not to encourage Luz to hold the girl or to thank her for feeding her, but an ambivalent flash of the hand to signal that he didn't give a damn what she did.

So Luz shook some blueberries into her hand and offered one to the girl. The baby took it between her corpulent thumb and index finger and held it curiously. She jabbered something and Luz stared at her, baffled.

The baby slapped at the duvet and jabbered again.

'"What is it?"' said Ray. 'She's saying, "What is it?"'

'What is it?' the baby said again.

'Berry,' said Luz.

The baby did not know berry.

'Here.' Luz took the fruit and split it in half with her thumbnail. Luz offered the vein-coloured, butterflied meat of the blueberry to the girl and she took it into her small mouth. Immediately the child grimaced, squenched her face up in revulsion and opened her mouth. Luz cupped her hand beneath her chin and the baby let the spitty fruit drop out. Luz tried a berry and found it a tasteless mucus. 'Sorry,' she said. Ray chuckled a little and the girl told him to shut up. Ray flinched. 'Shut up!' the baby said once more, gleefully. Luz said, 'Be kind,' her own mother's rule.

Ray asked, 'What's your name?'

The baby regarded him suspiciously and he asked again. Then the girl made a sound like *Ig*.

'Ig?' asked Ray.

The girl chugged, 'Ig, Ig, Ig,' like some small engine.

'Ig,' said Ray, laughing, and the girl laughed too and began to roll around on the concrete, saying, 'Ig, Ig, Ig, Ig,' her face still flecked with black bits of blueberry skin. Ray and Luz laughed and the baby – little dynamo, little showboat, little ham – rolled more furiously, going, 'Ig, Ig, Ig, Ig.' They were having a good time, the three of them.

Then, sudden as a ghost, the child stopped rolling and popped up and bounded back to her wretched encampment. Luz felt a great reservoir of joy drain from her.

Ray watched her go, too, saying finally, 'She's sweet.'

'I don't like those . . . people,' said Luz.

'What's wrong with them?'

Luz scowled at her Ray. 'They're high –'

'Everyone here is high. They're letting loose.'

Luz knew he didn't believe this. 'Something's wrong with them.'

'You're paranoid.'

'Don't do that to me. Having a drink doesn't make me an idiot. I know what I feel.'

'Oh stop,' he breathed. The feelings card held little sway with the Hoosier.

'Look at them. Please.'

Ray turned. They watched the girl skipping and hopping irregularly between her people. 'Keep looking,' Luz whispered, urgent with the fear that Ray would not see what she saw, burdened with the weight of his waiting. This was the last chance, she knew, the last he'd humour her this evening.

The girl got on all fours and crawled to the straw-coloured dog, pressing her plank face dangerously close to the mutt's. Ray was unfazed.

The child lost interest in the dog and crawled along the silt crust to the young man who had been serving as steward of the water bong. He sat cross-legged in the dirt. The girl put her head in his lap. Ray shifted and Luz felt his attention fading.

Just then the boy brought his hand down on the back of the child's head, not a blow but a grip. Palming her head, he pumped her face into his groin twice, three times. His friends chuckled and he did it again. This time he hoisted his free hand into the air, a bull rider's pose. The group howled as he mashed the baby's white-blonde head into and out of his crotch, then released her.

Ray recoiled. 'Jesus.'

The gesture sickened Luz too, because it was sickening, but also because it was so wholly validating that she felt she had somehow asked for it, willed it into being. She said, 'See?'

'We should get someone.'

'There's no one.'

'Red Cross.'

'They won't come down here. Even if they did. They'll talk to them and they'll tell them some story and Red Cross will leave and they' – she flung her hand toward the wretched gang – 'will leave.' Her hand hung in the air, trembling as if resisting the force threatening to pull this child back into the endless asphalt maze of the Valley. 'They'll take her away and we'll never see her again.'

Ray began to speak. 'Listen,' he might have said, but Luz nodded to the Nut, walking away. The little girl tried to follow, stumbling, and he said, 'Stay there.' Soon, the whole jaundiced entourage – bong, dog and all – receded in pairs or one by one along the corridor, disappeared into the swell of the raindance, leaving the baby sitting in the dirt with her collection of sticks and trash.

'Where are they going?' asked Ray.

Luz had no answer. 'Baby,' she called. The child lifted her pale head and came running. Her run was a marvel. Luz outstretched her arms and the baby regarded the pose a moment before she leap-

frogged onto Ray's legs. Ray released a sitcom groan, which delighted
the girl and sent her up and leaping again.

And so another nonsense game was in full swing.

Ray chided Luz – '"Baby." You're so creepy.' – but he entertained
the child with a bald joy. 'Where are they?' he asked, but Luz had no
answer. The three of them played at piling little anthills of sand in
each other's hands and then played at blowing them into oblivion.
They played at Ray lying still then popping his eyes open and saying
boog and the girl squealing for shelter behind Luz. They played at
arranging all Luz's hair to cover her face like a curtain. The girl
was a fiendish collector and loved nothing more than scouting the
canal for like things and depositing them with the adults. Thus Ray's
pockets filled with pebbles and dead sticks, while Luz's backpack
became a repository for dust-chalked plastic bags and small shining
sails of garbage. During her depositing the baby would sometimes do
her dynamo chant: 'Ig, Ig, Ig, Ig, Ig.' And when the child set off Luz
and Ray chugged it to each other, 'Ig, Ig, Ig, Ig,' laughing in their old
easy way.

An hour passed, then another and all the while there was no sign
of the Nut or anyone from his group. Ray asked, again and again,
'Where are these people?'

They noticed an eerie adult quality about the girl. She touched.
She moaned to herself. When depositing a specimen she often paused
to lay her hands on Luz or Ray. She favoured stroking Luz's throat
especially, a disquieting stroke that could be described by nothing so
truly as the word *sensual*.

'What is that?' Luz said, after the child had tromped off for
another mini-expedition. 'The way she *feels* everything.'

Ray nodded. 'It's like she's seeing with her hands.'

Night was full on now, though it was a night obliterated by the
bonfire thoroughly raging, letting off a chemical acridity where
someone had heaved in a sofa. Soon the girl – whom they had started
to call Ig – tired of her collecting and began to whine and mash her
fists into her eyes. Luz made a pillow of Ray's shirt and coaxed the

girl into lying down. She took up a corner of the duvet and burritoed it over Ig's soft body. There, the child fell into a fluttering sleep. In the distance a long, manic drum riff crescendoed, sending up trills from the partiers. Ig had been with them for hours now.

'We should have asked where they were going,' Ray said.

Luz swaddled the duvet over the sleeping girl more snugly, wishing for something more substantial to wrap around her, wishing she could free her from the putridity of the improvised diaper. She laid her hand on the bundle of Ig and rubbed softly.

'Maybe they're not coming back.' She said it nonchalantly – almost a joke – but she knew it was true. She had known it since they left.

Ray didn't laugh. He looked at the sleeping girl, unable or unwilling to hide his pity. 'Who just leaves their kid?'

'Maybe she's not their kid.'

Ray was quiet, though Luz could tell he had plenty to say. He was doing the dutiful stoic bit that so provoked her. Around them, people scrambled to set up camp where they could get a good view of the bonfire. Luz felt herself pulled taut with the urgency that had been distending in her since the girl crashed into her life. She was close to bursting and frantic to make Ray feel that bursting, too. She was desperate to make him desperate.

'How could someone do that?' she said.

'What?' said Ray.

'Hurt a little one.'

He frowned down at Ig and pushed Luz's hair back behind her shoulder. 'I don't know.'

'Ray,' she said, startled to find herself near tears. 'We're going to have little ones and they're going to be hurt.'

'Babygirl, don't get like this.'

'There's too much hurt in the world to be avoided. More than enough to go around.'

'You just do your best.'

She leaned into him and gripped the inner meat of his thigh. 'Then let's do it.'

He inhaled and stiffened. 'Do what?'

'Our best.'

Ray looked at her, miniature bonfires winking in his eyes.

'It's been hours,' said Luz. 'Maybe they wanted us to have her.'

'You didn't even think those were her people.'

'They abandoned her, Ray.'

'You sound like a crazy person,' he whispered.

'Don't say that.'

'You do. You sound crazy.'

'I'm not,' she said. Was that true? She had not been up to assessing her own fitness for some time. And yet, here she felt solid. Righteous. She peered fiercely into Ray's prophet eyes aflame. It had been a long time since she believed in anything. 'I cannot accept that there is nothing we can do. I won't.'

The drums pounded on and the bonfire swelled with mattresses and furniture and driftwood. There was a flare in the distance and an orb of yellow-white gaslight bloomed overhead. Then another flare, another fireball, another ripple of jolly pandemonium travelling through the canal. Ray said nothing.

Someone detonated a round of mortars, a purely sonic cluster of explosions which left pale smoke blossoms in the starless night and woke Ig. She startled in her bundle then sprung up, wailing. Luz tried to take hold of her but the girl scrambled away in terror. She stood on the smooth and cracked concrete infrastructure, shuddering with panic, her soiled diaper drooping between her bowed legs. More explosions came and Luz knew as she had known anything that the child was on the verge of tearing off into the darkness, through the dry canals to the channel that was once the Los Angeles River, streaking all the way to the black and infinite and worthless sea.

Suddenly, in one purposeful and athletic motion, Ray was off the blanket. He strode to the girl and scooped her into his arms. She wailed still but he pressed her to him and held her. He paced, jouncing the child lovingly and murmuring into her pale head. Luz tucked the hoodie around Ig and at the cacophonic arsenal of the bonfire's climax she pressed her hands over the child's small ears. It was useless, she knew, but Ray gave her one of his endlessly warm, instantly soothing smiles and she kept them there. Eventually Ig calmed, slackened and fell back to sleep.

The bonfire caved in on itself and the revellers followed. Soon, another ineffectual raindance would disburse up and out of the canal. Luz folded their blanket, packed the growler, berries and jugs in the backpack and donned it. Ray watched, Ig still in his arms, her glowing head draped over his shoulder. They stood looking at each other. Ray's eyes were reddish and bleary now and seeing them made Luz's hurt, too. She wanted to go home. She had the sense that they were standing on the edge of something and she wanted to step off, together.

Then, Ray's eyes widened.

Luz turned, looking for what Ray saw instead of her. Below, across the dark dry canal a serpentine figure moved easily through the churning crowd. He came toward them. The Nut.

Luz did not breathe. The berm was dense with people. It was possible the Nut had not seen them. They could flee. Ray froze but Luz leaned into him. She released two hard syllables, her truest: 'Go. Now.'

He went, swiftly, wordlessly, and she followed, through the throngs, up and over the berm. On the lip of the canal, Luz looked back, the bonfire a dying star behind them, the Nut coming at them, maybe.

'Here,' said Ray, pulling her through a gouged redwood gate dangling from its post by one hinge. They weaved through the lifeless backyards of the abandoned craftsmen, past shredded hemp hammocks, drained koi ponds, groves of decorative bamboo gone to husks and whispering *Easy, sweetheart*. Past upended kilns, pottery-shard mosaics, slashed screens, slivers of smashed Turkish lamps lynched from what had once been a lemon tree, bird-feeders still half filled with Shirley Temple nectar, wire skeletons of dissolved paper lanterns, splintering croquet mallets, terracotta pavers, disintegrating block walls, gutted cushions, a burnt-out miniature pagoda, a canoe filled with excrement and ancient newspaper. All the while, Luz watched the baby's glowing haloed head where it bounced on Ray's shoulder, nodding *yes yes*. It led her to the starlet's car, to Ray, and together he and she fled to their canyon, with their Ig. ■

© MIE MORIMOTO
from *pH*, 2013
Courtesy of Misako & Rosen, Tokyo

HOLIDAY

Mona Simpson

Any minute, a car-pool car will pull up with my youngest daughter. She is what I dress for now. I brush make-up around my eyes. I never fussed this much for any date.

But then, I've been married a long time.

A huge vehicle pulls to a stop and Mae springs out, the rock of a backpack on one small shoulder.

'Hey, Mom,' she calls, as nonchalant as if she'd grown up with a mother always waiting on the porch holding a young dog. She hasn't though. Until this year, I never arrived home before seven. We just got the puppy.

'How was school,' I say. Not really a question.

'Good. Fine.' Not really an answer. 'I have to go to the bathroom so bad.' The backpack falls with a thud and she runs.

One more minute to myself. I hug my legs and taste my breath coming back from my knee. I love the smell of skin. For three days I haven't called Ben Clerk. Props! (His word that I impressed my kids by knowing.) I give myself props, kiss my knee. All day long, I know where he is; I've memorized his rounds. But his shift is done, and after, I can't follow him. He's kept a curtain around his life at home. Here, on the other side of the city, the important part of my day is just beginning.

I sit on the porch steps in the mom uniform – jeans, Uggs and a sweatshirt. The puppy on a leash licks my ankle.

An hour ago, I reamed out the pharmacist. I'd asked for three small bags of total parenteral nutrition, so I could put them one at a time in the fanny pack under my sweatshirt and it wouldn't bulge so much. He sent me an enormous sack instead. 'It looks like I'm pregnant with a brick!' I said.

'You're rolling the dice with infection,' he answered. Of course, every time you detach and reconnect TPN, there's risk.

I've become discerning about pity. At first it made me snap back in shame. Now, I use it; the pharmacist finally relented: he sent over two medium-sized bags of the goop. The nurse jumped up from the couch when the delivery came, grateful for a task. Robby had interviewed six women and hired this nurse. His staying home had never been considered.

Only now, when dressing has become aerobic and you could argue that it's too late, do I really understand the importance of looks. Another lesson. My year has been a fucking staircase of lessons. I flash, guilty, on Robby's mother, once a beauty, now in the assisted living pavilion of Sunset Gardens. Robby and I used to joke about her vanity; now it seems a generosity, not easily maintained, to look a way that doesn't frighten children.

Less than a month ago, I learned to walk again with a chair.

Ben Clerk was the one who taught me.

Mae stands above where I'm sitting. I kiss her bare knee; she twists away. 'Wanna rollerblade?' Another not-real question. It's a test. Everything now is a test.

Buckling the tight in-line skates, I *appreciate* the late sun pressing my arms and remember the warm blankets in ICU. I'm going to google those heating machines. Keeping a grip on the puppy's leash, we sidestep down in the tippy skates and begin our eternal conversation. Every day, she tells me the names she plans to give her children. She is going to have two boys and a girl.

'I've changed up my arrangements. I like Charlie now. So it'll be

Oscar, Caitlin and Charlie. Not Spencer. Or Ryan. And I'm going to be one of the fun moms. After school I'll pick them up and do things.'

She skates in wide strokes, arms everywhere and no helmet. Since I've been back, I've let more things go. My phone rings. I look but don't answer.

'Who is it?'

'Ben Clerk.'

Mae already knows that he's Mom's favourite nurse.

Just his name on my phone loosens a rush of joy. 'And what will they be like?' I ask.

She thinks. This child, you can *see* her thinking. 'The boys will be really good at sports. They'll have bunk beds. And I'll make special kid meals, like pizza, unlike *some*one I know.'

Robby has been reading texts on Mae's phone after she's asleep. From this, we know that she's been kissed. Yesterday, she asked for a credit card to go shopping. She returned with three bras, thick with what used to be called padding.

'They're all like that,' she said, meaning bras.

Under the T-shirt, her breasts seem larger than mine.

There are still hours to wade through before bed. But then it will be four days since I called Ben Clerk. When I first came home, we'd talked twice a day. But even that hadn't been enough for me.

So I'm trying to wean myself.

The last time I tried to forget someone I was just a few years older than Mae and I made pledges in a spiral notebook: if I didn't call for ten days, I'd bake myself brownies with pecans and eat the panful. Thirty days would merit a new dress. But time didn't work. I didn't get over that boy until I met Robby.

This time, there'll be no getting over. I'll always want to call Ben Clerk. And eventually I will. But maybe I can stave off the longing for a while, in exchange for glittering days with my children. The flat long streets of our neighbourhood are good for rollerblading. Much of the time, we just coast.

I don't remember meeting Ben Clerk. He was always there, in the square room, which hangs by itself outside my real chain of days.

As in any intensive care unit, pain rippled through the air, but this time it was mine, no one else's. Terror of pain had made me pick ob-gyn twenty years ago. I'd wanted daffodils. Asian persimmons. Grey-blue ruffled baby bonnets. A reindeer hide on a white-painted nursery floor.

And I've had all those things. Now I want more – of course, everyone wants more. Even the dying. Green biology pushes up, even when the body fails.

I'd once thought sex was embarrassing – to be seen while your body moves out of control, seeking its own ends. But pain is worse. What the good surgeon administered to me in that square room was medicine distilled to a potent kernel.

Ben Clerk wrote down things I said, under the ether.

Remember when we were caught inside one of their animals?

I'd aspirated and one by one the systems began to close: lungs, stomach; only the heart trudged on. Robby brought the boys to say goodbye to me. The three of them stayed at a West Hollywood hotel four nights, leaving Mae with another family thirty miles west in Santa Monica. Robby thought she was too young to see her mother intubated. The boys stepped up to the hospital bed, tentative, white with fear. After their visit to my room, Robby found our oldest on his knees in the hospital chapel. A child who'd never been taken to any church or temple.

The good surgeon finally stabilized me on a respirator. For days, they wouldn't let me have anything, not even ice, while my throat throbbed raw, ragged with bright pain.

After Robby and the boys left, I begged the good surgeon, 'You have to trust me for the big big things. When I need a spoonful –'

The good surgeon's wife was divorcing him but there in the square room, the real arena of his life, he was a kind, patient man.

Those long nights, Ben Clerk replaced my blankets when the warmth drained. I tossed and woke, the heat melting onto my skin in flakes.

I want to buy one of those warming machines for home.

Ben changed the stiff sheets and cleaned me. One day he brought a bunch of dandelions in a Mason jar.

Another time, he carried in a fashion magazine. Who can afford this stuff? I asked, dishonestly. *I* could afford it, back in my life. But for doctors dresses are frivolity; every day I wore a lab coat. I'd never gone in for fashion. Maybe I would now.

Everyone can afford a new lipstick, Ben said.

Lipstick!

I didn't notice until I'd been moved to the rehab floor that he was young and bald. He was strong. He could easily pick me up. He did. I felt a quick stabbing uptake of air.

Opinions at the dinner table zing by, a ping-pong game I hardly follow. For months, I didn't read the paper. I've begun again; I try to stay alert to their concerns. But nothing sticks. Robby reads out local ballot propositions as the boys' voices climb over each other to be on top, the way their bodies once did. Dinner has lost all structure. We eat from tinfoil vats a UCLA girl delivers. Robby hired her too. There are no courses. Mae ignores the conversation and serves herself seconds and thirds of mashed potatoes made with butter and cream. She likes this new regime and is stocking up, in case we revert to my cooking. I used to carry home a string bag of Chinatown vegetables, take a few things out of the cupboards and touch the lemons in my bowl of garlic and ginger. I'd assemble the ingredients before starting. That moment of deliberation with my few elements spread, the small pot of rosemary on the windowsill, made a calm transition when I could cherish my life.

My sons interrupt each other. Have they always talked so fast, naming names that mean nothing to Mae and, now, to me? It's my fault; I've let them.

I suppose because I was relieved to follow my own thoughts.

All of a sudden, everyone is staring. I look up; did I do something –

'Mom, you lifted your fork halfway to your mouth and then put

it down!' My oldest, the love of my life, says, his long legs spread
out beyond the table. The casement window is flung open; we smell
the lawn.

I'm too skinny now. They blame me.

I try a lame joke. 'Remember when people thought I was dieting?'

'I know,' Mae says, speaking up for the first time during the meal.
'People asked me what diet you were on. Lexi's mom thought you
went to a spa.'

Decades ago, in a smaller California house, I'd agonized in front
of a mirror. I'd thought my jeans didn't look the way they were
supposed to. And they hadn't. I'd been right. Now, having lost my
hips, I understand jeans. Fashion is made for specific bodies. When
flat-chested women breastfeed and gain cleavage for the first time,
they all say they need new T-shirts.

I will have to learn to eat again. But I've lost desire for food.
Swallowing frightens me. Robby called my doctors from his office
and they told him there was no reason I couldn't eat. But I really
can't. For months they wouldn't let me and now it doesn't work any
more. Even my son doesn't believe me.

In the clean dry kitchen, pharmaceutical bottles wait by the sink.

Dusk accumulates in the sky.

How soon can I go to the bedroom and watch TV?

I listen to his message on my phone again. *Hey, checkin' in to see how
you are.* I don't call back. This must be what's called game playing.
But I like the temporary imbalance; I have a pass now, to call any
time. Crystals grow on that possibility.

Robby slides into the bedroom, his phone at his ear. He has a
speech impediment that has no name. It was the first thing I noticed
about him years ago; listening to his softened consonants, I knew I'd
always be comfortable with him. He sits on the bed, still talking, and
absently rubs my back, the way of the long married.

I'm googling for medical blanket warmers. A half-hour later,
I have to yank myself out of the laptop – where Jetsetter, an Internet

vacation site, has become my porn. I've ordered a blanket warmer. It will ship tomorrow.

Robby and I had our romance too, in Berkeley a long-ago spring, but I can't recall those emotions any more, I can't feel them from the inside. I don't remember holding myself back, the way I'm trying to now with Ben Clerk. Robby was always just Robby. There was no one else.

A massage board has been set up by the windows. Robby has hired someone to give him massages. He takes care of himself. I can almost imagine leaving it all. The family would keep moving without me. That feeling spreads in me, a calm vista seen from far away.

Tomorrow I'll be so busy I won't miss calling. I fall asleep thinking of Ben Clerk, allow myself that melt into dream.

The two doctors stand to clap when I walk in.

'They think I have an eating disorder,' I say.

'Maybe you do,' the oncologist says.

'No. I can't eat.'

The good surgeon calls the stomach guy. While we wait for him and for the radiologist, they ask how I'm feeling.

'The last time I was home all day was maternity leave with Sasha. I mooned around depressed even then. When can I go back to work?'

They want to look at today's scan before deciding.

The notion of return carries anxiety too. I've abandoned patients. They'll have questions. Five years ago, I left a private practice in a bungalow where an embroidered sampler hung on watery blue walls – *The eternal conspiracy of hush and clean bottles* – to treat immigrants downtown. I can do what I do, I said at parties, because my husband's salary pays our kids' tuitions. Robby's success is still a wonder. His parents' biggest fear came true; he never learned to work at school. But he loves the buildings he grew up around and has a knack for matching people with property. When I left our practice, my partner began to specialize in fertility and Robby sold the bungalow at a profit.

My patients work in sweatshops. Few hold green cards. They send their babies home, across the ocean, to their mothers.

'I'm afraid of nerve damage,' I say out loud.

'Some people steal prescriptions to get nerve damage,' the oncologist says. Is she trying to make a joke about SSRIs?

How long have you been smoking? she once asked me, looking at the picture of my lungs.

I never smoked, I said.

She said, Oh, you grew up in LA, then.

Every sub-specialty has its jokes.

'I can't survive another week at home,' I say.

'You may have to develop a hobby, Elaine.'

'I know,' I say. 'Maybe I'll take up smoking.'

I once loved our house. The smell of night-blooming jasmine slips in through dormer windows. We've owned the property seventeen years and never renovated, not the way people do here.

It had all mattered once – so much! – I remember, walking in, past the markers of that past life. I'd cherished a Japanese tea set, painted with willows. I found the cups in an antique store near the bungalow and then more pieces, separately over time, with deep satisfaction, though I'd never once, during the following decades, set them out to serve tea. The hooks of my old pleasures can't snag me now. I float around them, a round-edged ghost.

A text: Oh! I can go back to work.

Props.

Our first walks were in the hospital; I pushed a plain wooden chair in front of me down a corridor in the rehab wing. Then, one day, Ben lifted away the chair. I stumbled, but he righted me. On a weekend, I ate half a dish of oatmeal; I couldn't wait to tell him. This was my life: three steps then five, then eight. I couldn't say any of this to my family, except in an offhand way. They lived in a different realm and I wanted them to. Ben and I eventually took a field trip to the ground-floor cafe where the residents sat flirting on their coffee breaks, their giddy buzz heightened by exhaustion. The world tipped and I saw another life: these young doctors would never leave the world of illness. I hadn't wanted that.

Maybe now I do, I thought.

On the eighth day home, I return to work. I dread seeing patients who know me. I failed some who needed me after I promised to be there, no matter what. I'm fourteen pounds down from what I was then – and that was after two rounds of chemo.

By the end of the day, though, I'm back in.

I'd had my answers ready, true and breezy.

But no one even asked.

The women I'd seen in the bungalow would have demanded to know where I'd been. A few would have hired lawyers. But my immigrant patients accepted disappointment and didn't complain.

Day Fifteen, waiting for the car, I dial Ben Clerk. I can't drive yet. We had to hire someone for that too. Robby found a car service but I remembered a neighbour's son, home from rehab. He's happy to have a job and he's inconspicuous in my car. I want to hear Ben's voice. I crave that. Then he answers and it's thrilling but only quietly so – it also feels just normal, like my life. As if my life *is* quietly thrilling. We talk about nothing. We gossip about the good surgeon, who'd promised to visit his daughter at Scripps on parents' weekend. But a motorcycle accident delivered a new set of lungs. The surgeon's wife yelled like an insane person at the nurses' station. Ben names another patient. Caroline. When the car comes, I hold a hand up – the neighbour kid will wait – and tell Ben that every night I fall asleep thinking of him. 'You're just imaginary now,' I complain.

'Experience is overrated,' he says.

I could stand here listening to him forever. I love his voice. He finally says he has to go.

From then on, I let myself call. All the discipline, the self-control –

out the window, for these streaming glossy minutes on the phone. It's like skiing straight down.

My mentor, the top guy in the world for high-risk pregnancy, brings me a stick he calls the Alpenstock, which he used to climb mountains in Lebanon during medical school.

We walk slowly. 'I want to show you something.' I point the stick at a small house with a FOR SALE sign. 'I want that place.'

'And you would bring the nurse with you?'

I shrug. 'Until I don't need her any more.'

'When will that be?'

'Soon,' I say. 'As soon as I can eat. I'm working again. You think I'm crazy?'

'I do,' he says.

'I'm only forty-six.'

'That's on one side. On the other, you have three children. You weigh ninety pounds. Your bones show.'

'I don't even know what money's mine. He does that.'

He sighs. 'I remember your marriage. First, you have to gain your weight.'

'I'm trying.' I have a secret goal. I want to drive to see Ben Clerk.

'*How* exactly are you trying?'

'I drink something called Ensure. 360 calories, thirteen grams protein.'

'Is it tolerable?'

'Well, you can buy it at Rite Aid. The shelf life is eight months. That pretty much tells you all you need to know.'

Years ago, my mentor stomped into a lawyer's office and asked how much it would cost to divorce his wife. Then he'd done what we all do; he'd gone back to work.

'Whatever happened with that?' I ask.

'Too expensive,' he says. 'Where did you get the canine?'

'The pound.'

In ICU, there's something called the lipstick syndrome. Ben tells me, 'We know a patient's turned a corner when she starts asking for her make-up. If she puts on lipstick, she's ready to try.'

I call him from a store where I'm buying my mother-in-law tracksuits, a pile of soft cotton over my arm. 'She still doesn't know I'm sick. A virtue of dementia.' I don't say that she might outlive me.

'Have Robby put your pyjamas in the dryer,' he says. 'Bring them to you warm.'

'Pretty soon I can take baths. As soon as I get the tube out.' I say that easily to him. Around my kids and Robby, I don't mention the apparatus more than I have to.

Ben doesn't answer. I want him to cheer me on. It's a big thing, getting the tube out! Really big! Eating is hard! He knows that. I made myself chew walnuts last night; they're still in there. Two stones under my breastplate.

'There's a difference between wet warm and dry warm,' he finally says.

'What's the male equivalent of the lipstick syndrome?' I ask.

'Shaving.'

One day I leave a message and he doesn't call back for twenty-four hours. Then, when he does call, he can't talk long. The same with texts. The same with email.

I don't let myself sulk. Not the first week or the second. We're still talking, I tell myself. It's not all I want, but by now his voice is a drug I need.

While I'm drinking Ensure in the kitchen, my oldest leans in and asks for a sip.

'Not so bad,' he says. 'Give me one. I'll drink a can for every one you down.'

I apologized to the good surgeon the day he drove me home from the hospital. 'I may not make it, Doc.' He'd given me the most valuable thing a person can.

He had a calm smile. 'We all go sometime.'

I noticed the blue wrapped brick of folded clothes, ripped open on his back seat.

'But I have a young daughter.'

'That's why we're trying to buy you some years.' A holiday, in doctor talk. Oncologists don't talk of cures. They hope for holidays. 'Robby's a good guy,' he said.

He is. But maybe it's not goodness that I need now. Marriage is like chemo. Your first shot is your best shot. After that, you have to expect diminishing returns.

I'm the one who always calls. The oldest story in the book. Two married people. One goes back to his life. The other can't forget.

If only he still wanted me. My life is a radio song.

Ben first kissed me the week I was leaving. I'd imagined it too many times by then. He bit my lower lip. It felt like a sting, the way high-school boys zeroed in on you for the attack. I felt the expected remorse, not for Robby or my children – they were busy in their peregrinations – but for him. You'll have children, I said. You're just at the beginning.

I won't have children, he said.

The day I left, Ben sighed. People don't come back. Nobody wants to see her ICU nurse again. It's like being a divorce lawyer.

After work, I take a taxi to his hospital, text from downstairs and then wait. I haven't met my goal of driving yet. I may never. Some days I can eat, but only some. The feeding tube has been taken out, temporarily, and I'm already losing weight.

To see him – his face! – that's vast for me. I feel the way someone might after seeing a cliff. I could go home now. There's so much to assimilate. But he's holding car keys. 'Come on,' he says.

We ride in his old Honda. It's ridiculous, a person who looks the way I do, hoping for love, thinking about moving.

He takes me to his house and we sit at the small kitchen table, with only two chairs. It looks like the table I grew up around. Metal tubes. Vinyl upholstery on the chairs. His hand covers mine.

'I thought with these new lungs, I'd get ten years. Now I'll be grateful for five,' I say.

'You're much better,' he says. He means that. It feels like a badge. *Props.*

'I thought I could gain back to where I was.'

'Little by little. You're working every day?'

I nod. 'Can I kiss you?'

He leans down and then I blur – I'm not sure after, if it was ten minutes or thirty.

'I have a body now,' I whisper.

He looks perplexed. 'It doesn't feel quite right,' he says.

I'll think of that a hundred times, maybe a thousand. Had it not felt quite right to me?

At the moment I'm getting up to leave – my purse, the Alpenstock, my phone – I say, 'Every time I come back, first the chemo and now the surgery, I have a little less. How much less is too much, I keep asking myself. When is it not enough left?'

'Not yet,' he answers. In the car, we're in the posture of after. My head in the dent of his shoulder. 'You'll know when. And then you'll call me.'

I recognize this for what it is: an ending.

That night, I tell Robby. As I talk and watch his face, I remember our first disappointment. Robby and I were both going to be doctors. We'd care for farm workers. The Central Valley, we thought. But then he got a D in Organic Chemistry. When he told me, his face looked naked, as if his features had grown bigger. At nineteen, I realized I wouldn't leave him. I'd have to be the one to make money. I could do that; I knew how to study hard. The farm workers would have to wait. As it turned out, though, Robby didn't need my help. That was the last time I'd pitied him. He made money offhandedly from just *remembering* old buildings.

He doesn't look at me now. He crosses his arms. His shoulders slump.

'Did you have sex?' he asks.

'In the hospital,' I say. What we did inside that room was sex, but not a kind of sex I could have had before, before cancer, before middle age, before the feather stroke of death. 'I had practically no body. You know.' I shrug.

Robby looks at me appraisingly, a little surprised, maybe a tiny bit proud? Probably wondering: how could it have been, with a person who has a tube sticking out of her, ragged skin around it?

I'd asked Ben the same thing. He'd waited before answering. Like any other sex. Naked. Scary.

Robby walks over to the dresser and picks up his phone. He's scrolling. He finds a screenshot of a text our daughter sent to the boy who kissed her.

My mom got a new pair of lungs today.

He's not jealous, not exactly. It's different: he's frightened for the shape of our lives. All our lives. That would change without me, the way dinner had. The bones gone. But he would manage. In a smaller, separate compartment, he pities me.

Maybe pity is the form of love I can expect now. When I married Robby, he'd not been considered especially handsome. But his body has stayed the same and he moves well, into his late forties. He's kept his hair. Ben Clerk, at thirty-four, is completely bald. It's amazing how love changes you. I'd never noticed bald men. One bald man touched me, and now I see them everywhere.

'So what do you want?' Robby asks.

We've had an average marriage, full of minor complaints, daily contentment that had little to do with each other and fleeting crushes. But no close calls until now, when it's preposterous because the person confessing infidelity weighs ninety pounds.

When Robby had brought the boys to the hotel near the hospital, he'd risen early mornings and run ten miles in the Hollywood Hills, then showered before coming to the ICU, hair wet and health radiating an inch around him, a full-body halo. My oldest boy slept crumpled up in the chair by my bed.

Why did I tell Robby only after I knew it was over with Ben? It had been a long time since the majority of my thoughts and small goals and hopes and chagrins were communicable to him. I wanted to try.

But kids change pining.

At the stables, I watch Mae, a straight diagonal, on a piebald horse; she takes five jumps. Before we leave, I use the portapotty.

'I don't want to be one of those moms who has to pee all the time,' she says.

I refrain from saying, Then don't ever get pregnant.

We order salted caramel ice cream. I take a bite the size of a pea, let it melt on my rough tongue.

At home, I overhear Robby arguing with our son.

'It's your time for parties.'

'I've been out three or four times. There'll be more. I just don't feel like going to this one. When I have kids, she won't know them,' he says. 'I think of that sometimes.'

'She might,' Robby says.

'Probably not.'

I vow, just then, to try for his graduation. That will be my goal. I won't make it for Mae's. We all go sometime, said the good surgeon, who lives out of laundry in the back seat of his car.

On Jetsetter, I saw a picture of a family, each wearing Santa hats on the sand, in front of spotlit waves.

I'm back, I think, here.

I'll see Ben Clerk again, later. ■

SELF-PORTRAIT

Martin Amis

Brooklyn

My cat, Shadow, was at last getting friendly with his next-door neighbour, Benji.

At their previous convergences, of which there had been three or four dozen, Shadow and Benji squared up to each other like rabid hedgehogs; but all that hissing and bristling seemed to be safely behind them. Perched together on the wooden fence, both medium-sized and densely black, they brought to mind the twa corbies of the Elizabethan poem.

'So what's the set-up where you are?'

'Well, it's a tall house,' said Shadow. 'But I stick to the ground floor and the basement. The basement's where they put my crapper. Not that I use it much any more.'

'Nah. Do it outside and bury it.'

'Exactly. And dig the hole beforehand.'

'Common sense.'

Shadow turned his head. 'And the set-up where you are?'

'I'm in an apartment.'

'What's an apartment?'

Benji explained.

'Oh, a flat. Sorry. I'm English.'

'Yeah, I thought you talked kind of weird. No offence.'

'None taken,' said Shadow.

'So who serves the food at your place?'

'You see, the thing is there are four of them. Two smaller girls, one grown-up girl, and a man.' His eyes went wistful. 'The grown-up girl is the only one who serves me lovingly. Sometimes she even sings while she does it.'

'Sings?'

'Yes, sings. "He's the number-one boy in the world." That kind of song. The smaller girls serve me as if they're in some kind of hurry. And the man, he gags and groans as he does it – though at other times, I have to say, he can be quite considerate.'

'And, uh, the food itself?'

'Oh, all right I suppose. Savoury biscuits. Beef in gravy, chicken in gravy. Always gravy. And tuna and salmon in gravy. Shrimp. Sole. Mackerel. And sometimes real fish out of the fridge or the pan . . . What's all this about fish?'

'Yeah, exactly. Why do they think we like fish?'

'I know. Fish is *okay*. But what you really want is mouse.'

'Mm. Mouse is delicious,' said Benji. 'Mice are good.'

'Mm. When they're still warm. And the tail tickles your nose as you slurp it up.'

'And also they're fun to kill. But how often d'you come across a mouse?'

'I know. And they never *serve* mouse.'

Benji held up a forepaw and ran his tongue down it, as if for taste. 'You got a catflap?'

'What's a catflap?'

Overhead, twenty feet above Shadow and Benji, two female squirrels shimmied down the old telegraph pole and levelled out, Indian file, on the thick tightrope of the power line.

As she bobbed along the lead squirrel was saying, 'It's a good thing you've come. And I'll tell you why as soon as my friend joins us.

You'll like it here. It's not a big garden, as you can see, but just look at that. We happen to be quite proud of it.'

'Two *huge* boles. That's a serious tree. Do you know what kind it is?'

'Mulberry. So there's sometimes quite a bit to nibble on too.' Her head jerked sideways and downwards and she said, 'And don't worry about *them*. The one who's not licking his leg – that's the actual garden cat.' She gave an amused chirrup. 'The garden cat tries a pounce every so often. It's pathetic.'

'No speed.'

'No speed. None. I've seen grass grow quicker than that. I give him a good cawing too, every time he tries. The garden *man* would be quicker than that.'

'Him by the glass doors?'

'Yes, him. Mind you, there's no harm in the old boy. He's only having a smoke. Once in a while he's given me a fright, but nowadays I just ignore him. In fact he comes in useful – when the opossum skulks by.'

'You have an opossum?'

'Now and then. All he is is another lumbering trash-eater. He's no threat. Just horrible to look at. Like one big sore. And the old man there, he makes him slink off. Throws rocks at him . . . Ah, here she is.'

Another squirrel joined them.

'Now you girls say hello to each other and we'll begin.'

'Hello.'

'Hello.'

'Okay. As I said, I'm pleased we've found a third. Because you can do it with two but you really need three.'

'Need three for . . . ?'

'Tag.' She tensed herself into the *ready* position and her tail shot skyward. 'And you're it.'

'What's the stroking scene where you are?'

'Could be better, quite frankly, Benji,' said Shadow after a somewhat sorrowful pause. 'The smaller girls and the adult girl have a habit of picking me up. And I don't really like being picked up.'

'Me neither.'

'You feel trapped.'

'Right.'

'Out of your element.'

'Right . . . You know, it's good to find someone I agree with on this point. Getting picked up's overrated. How about the guy?'

'He doesn't pick me up, but he . . .' Shadow hesitated. 'Well, when I swoon onto my back at his feet and writhe around – completely irresistibly, I'd have thought – one time in *five* he'll bend down and give me a quick scratch under the chin.'

'And that's it?'

'Sometimes he just strokes me with his *shoe*.'

'His . . .' There was a troubled lull. 'Uh, Shadow, does your guy ever kick you?'

'Kick me? No. Certainly not. Why would he?'

Benji tipped his head this way and that. 'Yeah, well you see, my guy, he's always in a bad mood in the evenings. I say always. Nearly always. He comes home cranky. It's because he hates his job.'

'What's a job?'

On the paving stone beneath Shadow and Benji two flies were about to share a bird dropping – one that had taken the form of a crusty black splat.

The smaller fly was a freshly promoted pupa; indeed, on any reasonable timescale he was hardly out of maggothood. The taller and fatter and hairier fly was nineteen days old and, with any luck (if all went according to nature's plan), had about a week to live.

'Hey,' said the smaller fly. 'What goes on down there, old-timer?'

'That covered bit by the glass doors?'

'Yeah. I took a look. Trash can, woodpile. Damp and humid. Nice stink of butt smoke. Seems like a good place to go swarm.'

'It *is* a good place to go swarm,' said the older fly. 'Plus they got brightly coloured hosepipes and broom handles for you to glom onto. But know this, kid, and don't ever forget it. Whenever the man appears? Get the hell out of there.'

'Why's that, doc?'

'Because he's a mass-murdering bastard. That's why.'

The junior fly hawked out another jet of stringent drool to help liquefy his lunch. 'The swat?'

'Not the swat.' The senior fly paused for effect. 'The spray.'

The junior fly gave a gulp and said, 'The *spray*. I've dodged a swat or two in my time. As I told you, I usually hang out in kitchens. But the spray . . .'

'Look. Here he comes. Look. He stalks them and creeps up on them. Like he's on some kind of mission . . . *Jesus*. You see that?'

'Jesus. Right in the face.' The small fly gulped again. '*Now* what happens?'

'Yeah, watch.' The big fly's tone was grim. 'When they cop the spray they always take to the air and think they can fly it off. Then they're forced to land or they even crash . . . Yeah, he's down. Watch. See the wings flicker? And how he's trying to stretch his back legs? Kid, believe me, it's a terrible way to go.'

'Jesus.'

'Sometimes he's got *two* sprays. Two. One in each hand. The man's a fucking animal.'

'Point taken. You won't need to tell me twice.'

'I mean, haven't we got a right to exist – same as anybody else? He doesn't kill squirrels, he doesn't kill cats.'

'Ah, forget it. Life's too short.'

The senior fly was trying not to roll his compound eyeballs. He had a lot of time for the junior fly – but he did think that this kind of attitude was sadly typical of the younger generation. 'Come on, get serious, boy. Think. I mean, what are we? An inferior form of being? We don't sting or bite. Sometimes we buzz, but we don't whine – like others I could name.'

The small fly gave a dismissive upward flick with his pube-like foreleg and said, 'Yeah yeah.'

'Yeah yeah? *Think*, kid. Because I don't get it. I mean, what *is* it about us that's supposed to be so "offensive"? I don't get it. Can you name me one "distasteful" habit?'

'Fuck him. Eat up. Enjoy.'

For a while they conscientiously expectorated over their meal.

'Hey, old-timer, you know what?' The little fly swallowed with some gusto and said, nodding, 'This is good shit.'

'Later. I'll see you around.'

'A pleasure to talk to you, Benji.'

'Likewise. Hey, Shadow. How you going to get back in?'

'You've got your catflap, I've got my guy.'

Benji gave a sniff and said, 'Yeah that's right. He doesn't have a job. This asshole, all he does is let you in and out.'

'D'you mean arsehole?'

'We say asshole.'

'Well it's true. This uh, this asshole just lets me in and out. I'm always thinking, since he hasn't got anything else to do, why doesn't he stroke me more? But he's good at letting me in and out. I hardly ever have to wait. He's a full-time catflap.'

'Right. The asshole's a full-time catflap.'

Shadow smiled. 'You know, when he lets me in I say thanks.'

'How d'you do that?'

'It's halfway between a mew and a purr. Like this.' He gave a demonstration.

'Nice,' said Benji.

'Now watch.'

Shadow glided down the seven steps and sat expectantly in front of the glass. The door opened.

'Thanks.'

'Don't mention it.'

'Thanks again.'

'No thanks necessary, Shadow. Just doing my job. After all,' I said with a shrug as I returned to the desk, 'that's what I'm here for.' ∎

The Fair Fight by Anna Freeman

From a filthy brothel to the finest houses in the town, from the world of street fighters to the world of champions, *The Fair Fight* is a vibrant tale of eighteenth-century female boxers and their scheming patrons, of courage, reinvention and fighting your way to the top.

'A hugely exciting and entertaining novel, written with warmth, charm, authority and, above all, terrific flair. I loved it.' Sarah Waters

'A brilliant, bold and unforgettable debut. Freeman transports us to a history we'd never have imagined and makes it viscerally real.' Nathan Filer

Weidenfeld & Nicolson £12.99 | **HB**

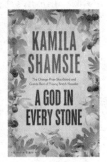

A God in Every Stone by Kamila Shamsie

July 1914. Young Englishwoman Vivian Rose Spencer is in an ancient land. Soon she will discover the Temple of Zeus, the call of adventure and love. Thousands of miles away, a twenty-year-old Pathan, Qayyum Gul, is learning about brotherhood and loyalty in the British Indian Army. Soaring across the globe and into empires fallen, this is the powerful new novel from one of *Granta*'s Best of Young British Novelists and Orange Prize-shortlisted author of *Burnt Shadows*.

Bloomsbury £16.99 | **HB**

Sworn Virgin by Elvira Dones

Hana Doda studies literature in cosmopolitan Tirana. Mark Doda is a raki-drinking, chain-smoking man in the Albanian mountains. They are the same person.

'The author puts a light touch on the issues of culture, immigration, gender tradition and race.' Harriet Addison, the *Times*

'Elvira Dones is one of the most distinguished Albanian authors writing today. Astonishing, brilliant and unabashed by taboos.' Ismail Kadare

And Other Stories £10 / $15.95 | **PB with French flaps**

Strange Weather in Tokyo by Hiromi Kawakami
Translated by Allison Markin Powell

Shortlisted for the Man Asia Prize and the Independent Foreign Fiction Prize, this international bestseller from one of Japan's most exciting literary voices is a touching story of modern Tokyo and old-fashioned romance. Tsukiko is in her late thirties and living alone when she meets one of her old schoolteachers in a bar. Gradually their friendship blossoms into something that might be closer to love.

Portobello Books £7.99 | **PB**

CONTRIBUTORS

Martin Amis's books include *Money*, *London Fields*, *Time's Arrow* and *Lionel Asbo*. He was one of *Granta*'s Best of Young British Novelists in 1983.

Anne Carson is a Canadian poet, essayist, translator and professor of Classics.

Diane Cook's first collection of stories, *Man V. Nature*, will be published by Harper in October. Her fiction has appeared in a variety of publications.

Anthony Doerr was a *Granta* Best Young American Novelist in 2007. His books include *The Shell Collector*, *About Grace*, *Memory Wall*, *Four Seasons in Rome* and, most recently, *All the Light We Cannot See*.

Aaron Huey's *Mitakuye Oyasin* won the 2014 Independent Publisher Book Award for photography. The second edition will be published by Radius Books in September.

Nicola Lo Calzo's photographs have been exhibited in museums throughout Europe, and published in *Newsweek*, the *Independent*, the *New York Times* and *Le Monde*, among others.

Thomas McGuane is the author of ten novels, including *The Sporting Club*, *The Bushwhacked Piano* and *Ninety-two in the Shade*. A new story collection, *Crow Fair*, will be published by Knopf in March 2015.

Andrew Motion was Poet Laureate from 1999 to 2009 and is co-founder and co-director of the Poetry Archive. His most recent poetry collection is *The Customs House*.

Melinda Moustakis's first story collection, *Bear Down, Bear North: Alaska Stories*, won the Flannery O'Connor Award.

Adam Nicolson is the author of several books about history, writing and the environment. His latest is *The Mighty Dead: Why Homer Matters*.

Prince Ofori-Atta is the editor of TheAfricaReport.com.

Jess Row was one of *Granta*'s Best of Young American Novelists in 2007. He is the author of *The Train to Lo Wu* and *Nobody Ever Gets Lost*. 'A Confession' is an extract from *Your Face in Mine*, published in August by Riverhead Books.

Mary Ruefle is the author of fifteen books of poetry and prose, as well as seventy-two erasure books. Her most recent work is *Trances of the Blast*. She teaches in the MFA programme at Vermont College of Fine Arts.

Mona Simpson was a *Granta* Best Young American Novelist in 1996. She is the author of six novels, including *Off Keck Road*, *My Hollywood* and *Casebook*.

David Treuer is Ojibwe from Leech Lake Reservation in northern Minnesota. His work includes three novels and a non-fiction book, *Rez Life*. His fourth novel, *Prudence*, will be published by Riverhead Books in 2015.

Claire Vaye Watkins's story collection *Battleborn* won multiple awards, including the Dylan Thomas Prize. 'Mirage' is an excerpt from a new project.

Callan Wink lives in Livingston, Montana. His stories have appeared in the *New Yorker*, *Men's Journal*, *The Best American Short Stories* and other publications.